W9-CSY-573

GREAT MOMENTS IN

GOLF

GREAT MOMENTS IN

GOLF

IAN MORRISON

GALLERY BOOKS
An imprint of W.H. Smith Publishers Inc.
112 Madison Avenue
New York, New York 10016

A Bison Book

Published by Gallery Books
A Division of W H Smith Publishers Inc.
112 Madison Avenue
New York, New York 10016

Produced by
Bison Books Corp.
15 Sherwood Place
Greenwich, CT 06830

ISBN 0-8317-4027-2

Printed in Hong Kong

1 2 3 4 5 6 7 8 9 10

Page 1: *Tom Watson fires an iron into the heart of the green.*

Pages 2-3: *Jack Nicklaus makes a rare visit to the sand during his record-breaking sixth Masters success in 1986.*

CONTENTS

INTRODUCTION

On Wednesday 17 October 1860 the first British Open was held over Scotland's famous Prestwick links. Willie Park senior emerged from a field of eight entries to become the first winner of one of the world's great sporting events. That, one could say, was the first great moment in golf.

Since then 126 years have lapsed and many great names have come and gone. It is therefore hardly surprising that, when faced with the task of picking out 30 or so great moments, it was difficult to know where to begin.

How one would have loved to have been at Prestwick in 1868 to see Young Tom Morris record the first hole-in-one at the British Open. A great moment I'm sure. But what was the reaction of the crowd?

Morris and his father brought their own magic to golf in the nineteenth century. Their presence on golf courses in England and Scotland regularly provided great moments, whether it be one shot, or a devastating round.

Just as those two dominated the early days of championship golf, three men did so at the turn of the century, and up to the first world war. Those three men became known as the 'Great Triumvirate' because, like the first great Roman Triumvirate of Caesar, Pompey and Crassus, they dominated the era. Between them they won 16 of the 21 British Opens between 1894-1914. How, with such domination, could they fail to produce a great moment or two?

The American breakthrough came when amateur

Above: *The 'home' of golf, St Andrews, where the headquarters of the Royal and Ancient are situated.*

Left: *The first greats of golf, the 'Great Triumvirate' of John Henry Taylor (left), James Braid (seated left) and Harry Vardon (standing). They are accompanied in the photograph by Scot Sandy Herd.*

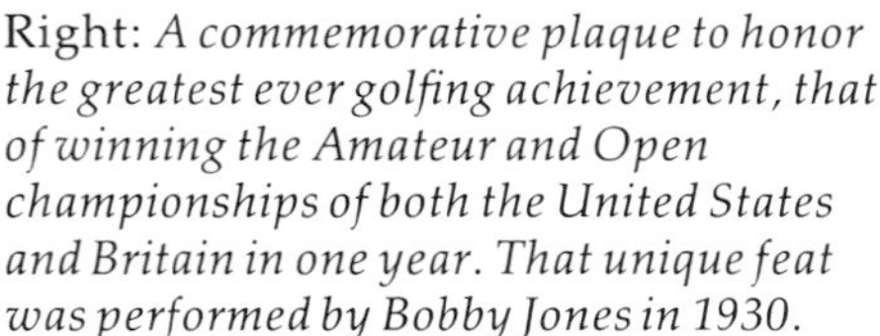

Right: *A commemorative plaque to honor the greatest ever golfing achievement, that of winning the Amateur and Open championships of both the United States and Britain in one year. That unique feat was performed by Bobby Jones in 1930.*

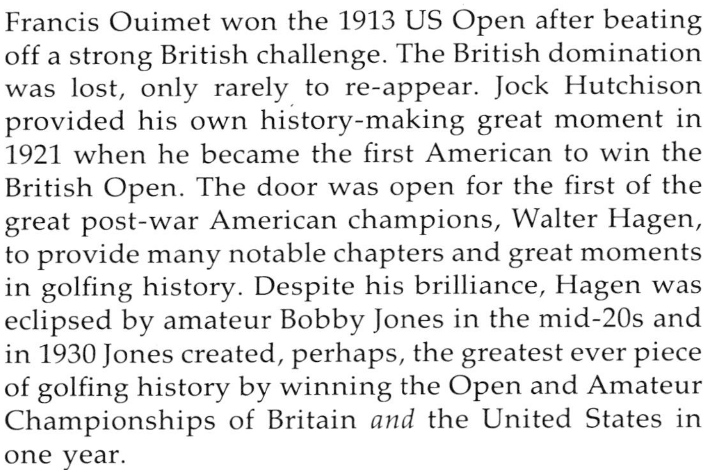

Francis Ouimet won the 1913 US Open after beating off a strong British challenge. The British domination was lost, only rarely to re-appear. Jock Hutchison provided his own history-making great moment in 1921 when he became the first American to win the British Open. The door was open for the first of the great post-war American champions, Walter Hagen, to provide many notable chapters and great moments in golfing history. Despite his brilliance, Hagen was eclipsed by amateur Bobby Jones in the mid-20s and in 1930 Jones created, perhaps, the greatest ever piece of golfing history by winning the Open and Amateur Championships of Britain *and* the United States in one year.

Many greats have tried, and failed, to win just the Opens of each country in the same year, thus highlighting the magnitude of Jones' performance. One man who did emulate Jones and win both Open championships in the same year was Ben Hogan in 1953. Hogan had a great contemporary in the early years after the war – Sam Snead, and they showed a dominance not seen since the days of Taylor, Braid and Vardon. They were followed in the sixties by another great trio – Palmer, Nicklaus and Player – who became known as The Big Three. If great moments in golf are sought, one could start and finish with those three. Each has written his own piece of golfing history in the 25 or so years since he first appeared on the scene. Palmer and Player are still delighting crowds with their play on the US Seniors circuit, while Nicklaus is still regularly seen on the US PGA circuit. Not only that, he is still winning, and still providing golf with great moments. As long as Jack Nicklaus can swing a golf club, there is every chance he will produce something special.

Spain's Severiano Ballesteros and West Germany's Bernhard Langer have launched an assault on the US Tour in recent years, and have certainly proved themselves as worthy challengers to the Americans on home soil. The likes of Trevino, Watson and Irwin have had to succumb to the Europeans who have both created their own great moments of golf.

Starting a list of great moments is simple. The list of the above mentioned great champions makes that job easy. The hard part is knowing where to stop. The great moments that follow have been particularly chosen to incorporate as many of the great champions, and as many eras as possible.

No two people could agree on a list of all-time-great golfing moments. It is therefore to be expected that you will disagree with some selections. But, whether you agree or not, I am sure you will find that each selection is, somewhere along the line, one of golf's great moments.

Far left: *Francis Ouimet (left) the man who opened the door for all American golfers by beating the powerful British pair of Harry Vardon and Ted Ray in a play-off for the 1913 US Open at Brookline. Bobby Jones, seen with Ouimet, was one of the men to help stamp America's dominance on the game in the 1920s.*

Left: *The second 'Great Triumvirate' of Jack Nicklaus (left), Arnold Palmer (center) and Gary Player.*

Right: *Two golfing legends Sam Snead (left) and Gene Sarazen seen about to tee off for the 1985 Masters – 50 years after Sarazen won the title. Their combined age in 1985 was 156!*

Below: *Tom Watson (left), Arnold Palmer and Jack Nicklaus (right). Watson was heir apparent to Nicklaus' throne, but the Golden Bear does not give up easily and in 1986 was still winning major tournaments.*

THE PRE-WAR YEARS

On a cold and dreary September day in 1913 a 20-year-old, unknown outside Massachusetts, took the golfing world by storm and opened the door for United States golfers to dispel the theory that the best golfers were of British origin.

British golfers had not only dominated their own Open championship since it started, but had also dominated the US Open since its first playing at Newport, Rhode Island in 1895. Johnny McDermott, in 1911, was the first home-bred American to win the title, all other winners having come across the Atlantic to compete, or were ex-Briton's domiciled in the States. When McDermott won his first title in Chicago, and then retained it the following year, the cream of the British professionals were missing. But when a record field of 170 gathered for the 1913 championship leading Britons Harry Vardon and Ted Ray were in the field. The presence of many other overseas players spurred the home-grown talent to enter, including a large contingent of amateurs.

Vardon, five times winner of the British Open, and his great contemporary John Taylor, had competed in the 1900 championship and they had been first and second, Vardon beating the third man, David Bell, by nine strokes. Now much older, Vardon's advancing years were more than compensated for by his great skill and he and Ray were expected to win the Open with ease.

Because of the large number of entries, two days of qualifying tournaments, each over 36 holes, had to be held on the Tuesday and Wednesday before the start of the competition proper. Harry Vardon headed the first qualifying group with a 36-hole total of 151. Just one stroke behind him was the unknown 20-year-old from Massachusetts, Francis Ouimet.

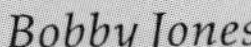

Bobby Jones

Walter Hagen

Harry Vardon

Francis Ouimet

OUIMET RE-WRITES GOLF HISTORY

Ouimet, who had won himself a lot of admirers following his performance against Jerome Travers, the eventual winner, in the recent Amateur Championship at Garden City, New York, lived virtually across the street from the Brookline Country Club, venue for the 19th Open, and came through the first 18 qualifying holes as the leader with a 74 to Vardon's 75. During the afternoon session he astounded his followers by taking a two-stroke lead over Vardon on two occasions but he came to grief at the 14th and lost the chance of a notable victory, albeit in the qualifying competition. Ted Ray won the second day's qualifying event, also over 36 holes, and it was down to serious business on the Thursday when the first 36 holes of the 72-hole championship were scheduled.

Although short, at 6300 yards, the Brookline course offered its rolling landscape with a background of chestnut and oak trees. Its velvet-like greens were not easy to read, and 150 bunkers were awaiting the less-than-accurate shot. Long hitting was expected after the summer's drought, and all-in-all conditions favored the two outstanding Britons.

Harry Vardon shared the lead after the first 36 holes with fellow Briton Wilfred Reid and they enjoyed a two-stroke advantage over Ray and Inwood professional Herbert Strong. Ouimet was partnered with Royal Ottawa's Karl Keiffer and, after a disappointing morning round of 77, completed his afternoon round by playing consistent and steady golf for a 74 and total of 151, the same score as another Open debutant, Walter Hagen – who was to dominate professional golf in the United States for nearly 20 years. Ouimet could well have been up with the leaders had he not had sixes at the first two holes of the day.

Ouimet played the final 36 holes with the 1909 Open champion George Sargent and the youngster returned a 74 for the first 18 in one of the coolest displays of golf ever seen in the Open. Ray had a 76 and Vardon a 78 which meant all three were level on 225 with one round to go, and Ouimet was the only American left to pursue the two Britons as the home-bred professionals failed to keep up with the British favorites.

The afternoon session was played in rain and muddy conditions and few really believed Ouimet could sustain his challenge against two men both old enough to be his father but, when the Brookline fans realized victory was a possibility they massed in their thousands around him as he went from hole to hole. At the end of 63 holes, and having just completed the last nine holes in 43 'thanks' to two sixes, all looked lost for the 20-year-old as he needed a 36 on the inward nine to force a play-off.

As he started his charge over the last six holes he had gathered a gallery in the region of 5000, all of whom seemed

Above: *Harry Vardon (driving) was surprisingly beaten by the unknown Ouimet in the play-off for the 1913 US Open.*

Left: *The man who re-wrote golfing history, Francis Ouimet.*

Right: *Ouimet at Sandwich during the 1914 British Amateur championship.*

to want a glimpse of, or to touch, their new hero. When Ouimet stood on the 13th tee he had to play the last six holes in two-under par to force a tie with Vardon and Ray who had both finished their rounds on 304. He got a birdie at the 13th and then parred the next three. He had just two holes left in which to make up one stroke for the tie. A three at the 17th was enough to put him level with Vardon and Ray and the cheer that went up could have been heard for miles around and the scenes were reminiscent more of a baseball match than a golf tournament. The like had never before been seen on a golf course.

At the 18th, Ouimet had a 35-footer for the title. The ball rolled past by three feet and he had a tricky-looking return putt. After rolling around the hole for an inch or two, the ball dropped in the cup, and the cheering started again. You would have thought the title was won. No matter what the outcome of the 18-hole play-off the next day, Ouimet had done enough to show that the best of British golfers could be thwarted.

Despite Ouimet's great display on the Friday, big money was still going on Vardon and/or Ray to take the title after the play-off, but those who foolishly invested their money on the overseas visitors did not account for the nerve of the young local lad. He had not only outplayed, but also outnerved his more illustrious opponents in front of an 8000-strong gallery that followed the trio over their last 18 holes.

Never more than a single shot separated the three men at any stage during the outward nine as Vardon and Ray failed to shake off Ouimet. Vardon was the first to take an outright lead at the sixth and he held it for two holes until all three drew level and remained all-square at the half-way stage on 38. Ouimet was first to strike on the inward nine with a three at the 10th when both Vardon and Ray made four. He extended that lead to two shots at the 12th but was pegged back by Vardon at the next.

of the truly great American professionals, Walter Hagen. Ouimet remained an amateur throughout his career and was to win the Amateur title again in 1931 and appear on the American Walker Cup team 12 times. One of America's best-loved golfers, he did much for US golf both at home and

Left: *Britain's Ted Ray, who was involved in the play-off for the 1913 US Open.*

Right: *Harry Vardon (left) and Ted Ray . . . both upstaged by Ouimet.*

Below: *Ouimet 'practicing' on the roof of London's Savoy Hotel, complete with hat and bow tie.*

Ray's chance went at the 15th when he needed two shots to get out of a trap after becoming the first of the three to find sand all day. But Ouimet was still keeping up with Vardon, or perhaps it should have been the other way round for the best golf was definitely coming from the American and it was Vardon who was struggling to keep up with the youngster.

As they stood on the 17th tee Ouimet was on 65, Vardon on 66 and Ray out of it on 70. Then, the championship was won as Vardon found sand and Ouimet holed a long putt for a three. He was three up going to the last and he extended that lead to five shots thanks to a four to Vardon's six.

The scenes at Brookline were unbelievable as American golf made its greatest breakthrough. The fans mobbed Ouimet and he was carried shoulder high to safety. And in reply to a question from a small lady, who had forced her way to the front of the huge crowd, Ouimet answered: 'I'll be home shortly, mother.'

No golfer could have beaten Ouimet on the day, or over the entire tournament, he won with skill. There were no demands on 'lady luck', he made all his own luck as he earned a place alongside Harold Hilton and John Ball as one of the world's great amateur players. More important, Ouimet re-wrote American golfing history and his win was to have a lasting effect as it proved that American golfers were capable of taking on, and beating the world's best.

Ouimet proved his win was no fluke when he won the Amateur title and French amateur title the following year, as well as finishing joint fifth in the US Open at the Midlothian Country Club, Illinois, behind the first

internationally and in 1951 he became the first non-British golfer to be honored with the captaincy of the Royal & Ancient Club at St Andrews.

The performance of Francis de Sales Ouimet at Brookline that September day in 1913 caused many notable scribes to pen new headlines and adjectives. Bernard Darwin, grandson of Charles Darwin and golfing correspondent to *The Times* of London, wrote: 'It was one of the most momentous of all rounds because, in a sense, it founded the American golfing empire.' The London *Weekly Dispatch* carried a front page lead which read: 'Is British sport to suffer a total eclipse?' . . . they certainly foresaw the future.

THE DOOR IS OPENED

Finishing joint fourth, just three strokes behind Vardon, Ray and Ouimet that day at Brookline was another 20-year-old American. But, because of the adoration bestowed upon Ouimet, few took much notice of this other youngster from Rochester, New York. That youngster was Walter Hagen who went on to succeed Ouimet as champion and then become the first American golfing legend as he dominated professional golf in the United States until the late 1920s.

Walter Hagen brought much more to golf than his great mashie play and putting stroke; he was an innovator. He is credited with giving the plus-fours to golf and he always dressed immaculately on and off the course – his famous camel-hair coat was copied by thousands up and down the States in an attempt to follow Hagen's style. His lifestyle matched his appearance and the twice-married Hagen rarely went to bed if there was action still going on around him. He often turned up for a match dressed in a tuxedo, but his lack of sleep rarely detracted from his style of play. Hagen was a winner, and he was capable of turning apparent defeat into victory.

Hagen's greatest contribution to golf, however, was convincing fellow professionals that they were not to be treated like lepers, that they were world-class entertainers and sportsmen. While few could copy Hagen's lifestyle they were made aware of their standing. Hagen fought for their rights and got clubs in America and Britain to respect them, rather than treating them like second-class citizens. To that end, all current professional golfers owe Walter Hagen a debt. Before Hagen's time professionals usually had to use tradesmen's entrances to clubs and were not allowed to use changing rooms, or eat and drink in the clubhouse bar. Hagen broke down that barrier and soon professionals were welcomed with open arms as Hagen took his, and the sport's image, to every country in which the game was played, enthralling galleries wherever he went.

Affectionately known as 'The Haig' he had a great personality and had the ability to mix with people at all levels, whether it be the man-in-the-street or royalty and nobility. The Prince of Wales (later King Edward VIII and Duke of Windsor) was known as 'Eddie' to Hagen and he regarded it as one of his greatest honors to have once held the flag for a Walter Hagen putt. A friend of the heir to the British crown could not be left out of a clubhouse bar or changing room.

Born on 21 December 1892 the son of William and Louise Balko Hagen, Walter picked up his first golf club at the age of five. He was caddying by the time he was nine and spent a great deal of his time in the pro's shop at the Rochester Country Club. When he was 11 he broke 80 for the first time and it was then apparent that Rochester had something special on its hands. After

Above left: *A young-looking Walter Hagen (photographed in 1919) – the first of the American golfing giants.*

Left: *Gene Sarazen, seen with his wife, was one of Hagen's great rivals in the 1920s.*

Above left: *Walter Hagen (left) and the English Walker Cup player Cyril Tolley during practice for the 1924 British Open.*

Above: *Ernest Whitcombe, runner-up to Hagen in the 1924 British Open at Hoylake.*

Left: *Gene Sarazen teeing off at the 1st at Hoylake.*

High School, Hagen had a chance to play baseball for the Philadelphia Phillies but decided to concentrate on his golf. He made his competitive professional debut in that famous US Open at Brookline in 1913 and just a year later, when only 21, he won the first of his two US Open titles.

At the Midlothian Club, Illinois, in 1914 he shot a first round 68, an Open record, despite a stomach upset as a result of over-indulgence in oysters and lobster. He led the tournament from start to finish to beat off a challenge from amateur Charles Evans by one stroke. His second US Open title was in the first post-war championship, at Brae Burn in 1919, when he played the last six holes in one under-fours to tie Mike Brady before beating him by one stroke in the 18-hole play-off. After winning the title a second time Hagen gave up his job as Oakland Hills professional to become a full-time tournament professional.

As the 1920s came, so did the golden age of American golf with Hagen dominating the professional game and Bobby Jones the amateur game. Hagen had later to live in the shadow of the great Jones but, in 1921 Hagen won his first PGA tournament and earned the title of undisputed match-play champion. (The PGA only became a stroke-play tournament in 1958.)

Hagen beat Jim Barnes, with whom he had played in an exhibition match on his first visit to Britain in 1920, in his first PGA final, at Inwood, New York, to become the first American-born winner of the title. That win started a seven year dominance of the title by Hagen and Gene Sarazen. Hagen lost to his great rival Sarazen in the 1923 final and that was his last defeat in the championship until Leo Diegel beat him in the third round in 1928. In between he won the title with wins over Jim Barnes, again, Bill Mehlhorn by 6 & 5, Leo Diegel and Joe Turnesa to create an all-time PGA Championship record of five wins, only equalled by Jack Nicklaus 53 years later.

One great example of Hagen, a master of gamesmanship, at his 'best' – or worst – was in the 1926 final against Diegel at Salisbury, New York. Hagen gave Diegel missable six-foot and eight-foot putts early in the match, but when, with the pressure on towards the end, Diegel turned to Hagen and asked for a simple two-footer, Hagen turned and walked away. Diegel thought there must be some undulations on the green he had missed and

Top: *The immaculately dressed Hagen being watched by Archie Compston.*

Above: *Hagen with caddie J.W. Williams at Moor Park in 1928.*

Right: *The great crowd-pleaser; Hagen after receiving the British Open trophy from A. Robertson-Durham of the Honourable Company of Edinburgh Golfers following his win at Muirfield in 1929.*

he lined up the putt to see it go by the hole. Hagen went on to win 5 & 3.

Hagen would regularly ponder over the easiest of shots either to fool his opponent or to earn extra applause from the gallery who would be led to believe the shot was a tricky one. That was the showman side of Hagen.

In the 1927 PGA Championship, although not on his best form, he had a brilliant competition when he was behind for most of the final against Joe Turnesa before eventually taking the lead at the 31st and going on to win by one. He was not going to enter the competition at all but dragged himself away from his fishing trip in Wisconsin and picked up a club for the first time in weeks. He had the change of mind when it dawned on him that if he did not play, the unfortunate winner would have to live with the 'he wouldn't have won if Hagen had played' remarks. So he played for the winner's sake ... and won himself!

Although Hagen finished an inconspicuous 53rd out of 54 in his first British Open in 1920 he delighted the British fans with his play at St Andrews in 1921 before returning the following year to Sandwich to win the first of his four titles, by one stroke from George Duncan and Jim Barnes. He became, once more, the first American-born winner of a major title although Scottish-born Jock Hutchison was the first man to take the coveted trophy to the States the previous year. The extrovert Hagen typically gave his entire first prize, equivalent to $500, to his caddy.

Arthur Havers restored some British pride by winning the 1923 Open at Troon but after that the American invasion was well and truly on. Hagen won his second title in 1924 when he needed a four on the last hole to edge out Ernest Whitcombe. He had a six-footer for his four, and the Championship. He hit it, turned to his caddy, threw him his putter and waited for the crowd to confirm what he already knew – that the ball was in the hole. It was, and Hagen won the title by one

stroke. Jim Barnes maintained the American domination of the British title in 1925 and then saw the emergence of the great Bobby Jones.

Jones' record is legendary and many comparisons were made between him and Hagen. Jones was certainly the perfect golfer while Hagen had the habit of getting into trouble off the tee, but recovering with devastating mashie shots and great putting. But comparisons are unfair. Both were great, but once Jones arrived on the scene Hagen had often to live in the shadow of the amateur from Atlanta.

Having won the British Open in 1926 and 1927, Jones did not enter the next two years and Hagen emerged as victor on both occasions. But would it have been a different story with Jones in the field?

Hagen had to beat off Gene Sarazen and Archie Compston at Sandwich in 1928 and a year later he won by six strokes from fellow American John Farrell. Shortly before his 1928 win Hagen was thrashed in a 72-hole match-play challenge by Compston at the Moor Park club when the Englishman built up a four-hole lead after the first 18 holes which he extended to an amazing 14-hole lead at the half-way stage. The match ended at the 55th hole with Compston the winner by 18 & 17. Hagen played below his best over those two days, but it was certainly the most embarrassing defeat in the career of the world's greatest match-play golfer. He did, however, gain his revenge three months later when he beat Compston 6 & 5 over the Sandy Burr Country Club, Massachusetts and the Westchester Biltmore course at Rye, New York.

In all Hagen won 11 professional 'Majors', a record that stood until beaten by Jack Nicklaus. But, despite winning five PGA titles, four British Opens, two US Opens, plus five Western Opens, Hagen always maintained the one match that gave him his greatest thrill was against Bobby Jones in 1926.

There were many who felt Jones was number one and Hagen number two. The flamboyant Hagen wanted to prove them wrong. He had the match arranged with 36 holes over Jones' course at Saratoga and 36 over Hagen's own course at St Petersburg. Hagen led by eight holes after the Saratoga leg, and went on to clinch victory on 'home soil' by 11 & 10. It would have been easy for Hagen to gloat in victory but he lavished nothing but praise on his opponent. But deep down Hagen knew he had proved to many that he was the king of American golf, albeit a disputed title.

Hagen retired from serious competitive golf in 1929 because 'he could not stand the thought of shooting an 80' but he came out of temporary retirement to win the 1931 Canadian Open and his fifth Western Open the following year, at the age of 39. He also played in the 1935 US Open, finishing third, just three shots off the lead. Hagen was also honored with the captaincy of the first seven US Ryder Cup teams, as playing captain in the first five, and non-playing captain in 1937 and 1947.

When not playing competitive matches Hagen delighted in taking his skills around the globe in a series of exhibition matches. A regular companion was Australian trick-shot expert Joe Kirkwood. The pair of them took golf to the masses to show it was a game that could be played by the man-in-the-street, and it was not just a game for the idle and the rich.

It is estimated that Hagen's earnings from golf were in excess of $1 million and he spent it as easy as it came. Once, while on tour in Canada he collected $3000 for the tour and, on leaving his hotel told the manager to open his best whisky and fill the baths with champagne and ale. He returned to the States with less money than when he had left!

After ending his playing days Hagen's only connection with the sport, apart from his social interest, was as head of the Walter Hagen Division of the Wilson Sporting Goods Company. He took the time to enjoy his two pastimes, hunting and fishing and, in 1956, published *The Walter Hagen Story*. He had to give up playing altogether after a heart complaint and then, in 1964 had a cancerous larynx removed. But he was often seen in club houses at big tournaments, hardly able to talk, but still acknowledging the 'thank yous' of the many professionals who never forgot the debt they owed Walter Hagen.

Walter Hagen died on his Traverse City, Michigan, estate on 6 October 1969 at the age of 76 and Arnold Palmer perhaps summed Hagen up best when, at a testimonial dinner in 1967 on one of Hagen's last public appearances, he said: 'If it weren't for you Walter, this dinner tonight would be in the pro-shop not the ballroom . . .' Ouimet had opened the door for all American golfers, Hagen had jammed it open, and a procession of greats has followed him through ever since.

Left: *Walter Hagen showing how to get out of a bunker.*

Right: *Hagen not only brought his own style of play to the game, but also his own style of dress.*

America's Second Legend

How fortunate America was to possess two golfing legends during the inter-war era when Hagen and Bobby Jones took advantage of Francis Ouimet's lead and paved the way for the first Golden Age of American golf.

Jones, born in Atlanta and ten years Hagen's junior, first came to prominence in 1919 when he reached the final of the US Amateur title as a 17-year-old, only to lose 5 & 4 to S. Davidson Heron. Jones had first played in the championship at Merion at the age of 14, but he did not collect his first title until 1924 when he beat George Von Elm in the final after beating Ouimet 11 & 10 in the semi-final.

By the time he won his first Amateur title, Jones had left his mark on the US Open in 1923 by beating Bobby Cruickshank in a play-off and leaving all the home-bred professionals in his wake.

Jones, holder of degrees in law, engineering and literature, never turned professional as he concentrated on his Atlanta law practice, but in the ten years between 1920-30 he was uni-

Above: *George Von Elm was Bobby Jones' victim when Jones won his first Amateur title in 1924.*

Below: *A large crowd watching Jones at St Andrews . . . and that was only for a practice round!*

Above: *Bobby Jones (back row, second left) with his fellow American Walker Cup players who beat Great Britain 10-2 at Royal St George's, Sandwich, in 1930.*

Left: *Jones getting himself out of trouble during the 1930 British Open at Hoylake.*

versally regarded as the greatest player in the world – but don't tell Walter Hagen! Bobby Jones was the perfect golfer, he had all the shots and the model swing. For an amateur to dominate world golf the way he did was, at the time, unthinkable, but few would have denied Jones his accredited status of 'world's greatest golfer.'

Jones retained his Amateur title in 1925 and then, in 1926, became the first man to win the British and US Opens in the same year. At Royal Lytham he beat Al Watrous by two strokes, with Walter Hagen four behind in joint

Left: *Horton Smith, the first Masters' winner, looked unbeatable after two rounds of the 1930 US Open but Jones knew better.*

Below: *Macdonald Smith who finished runner-up to Jones in both the British and US Opens in 1930.*

third. Jones played one of golf's great shots out of a bunker at the 17th when he hit a mashie shot that landed inside Watrous' ball, already on the green. A plaque to commemorate the shot can be found in the face of the bunker at Royal Lytham. He completed the historic double at Scioto, Ohio, with a one-stroke win over Joe Turnsea. Jones came close to an unprecedented Grand Slam of the Open and Amateur titles of both countries in 1926. But defeats in the final of the US Amateur by George Von Elm, who thwarted Jones' attempt to win three successive titles, and a sixth round knockout in the British Amateur championship, ended such hopes.

Jones won his third US Amateur title in 1927 as well as returning to Britain to win the Open at St Andrews with a new championship record of 285, six shots ahead of Aubrey Boomer. He continued his run of winning a major title each year in 1928 when he beat British Amateur champion Phil Perkins 10 & 9 in the US Amateur Final. That run of success was extended in 1929 as Jones beat off the cream of American professionals including Gene Sarazen, Densmore Shute, Tommy Armour, and Al Espinosa, who Jones beat in a 36-hole play-off, to win his third US Open title. But all Jones had done before was completely overshadowed the next year as he clinched the Grand Slam of Open titles and Amateur titles of Great Britain and America – the Impregnable Quadrilateral as this seemingly impossible feat was described.

GOLF'S GREATEST ACHIEVEMENT

Just as Francis Ouimet had re-written golf history in 1913 so too did Bobby Jones in 1930 when he performed the greatest ever golfing achievement in the four months between May and September of that year.

Jones had never won the British Amateur title and, of the four he was to contest in 1930, it was the one he wanted more than any, all the more so since it was played at St Andrews, a course that Jones loved. In return the people of St Andrews loved Jones and were anxious for him to win the title.

Apart from the odd close call, against Cyril Tolley in the fourth round and fellow Americans Harrison Johnston and George Voigt in the sixth round and semi-final, Jones had little difficulty in reaching the Final. Once he had reached that far there was no stopping him and he left Britain's Roger Wethered wondering what hit him as Jones ran out the easy 7 & 6 winner. With the first leg of the Grand Slam safely won, the Hoylake course was to be the scene of Jones' next triumph as he went on to win his third British Open title.

Fred Robson was the only Briton to offer a challenge to the American visitors as Leo Diegel, Macdonald Smith, Horton Smith and Jim Barnes all played second fiddle to Jones who won by two strokes. After a three week lay-off Jones arrived at Interlachen for the third leg of the Impregnable Quadrilateral, the US Open.

Jones had not been playing his best golf in Europe and was having some difficulty with his woods, but when he shot a 71 in the opening round at Interlachen, it was apparent any such discord was well and truly resolved. Jones effectively won the title in the third round with a devastating 68 to the 76 by tournament leader Horton Smith. He could well have lost the tournament had it not been for that great third round because he had a mixed final 18

Below left: *The smile says it all as Jones collects the British Open trophy; the second of four collected in 1930.*

Below: *Wherever Jones played he attracted a large gallery, just as he did at Hoylake in 1930.*

Above: *Bobby Jones (right) with Roger Wethered before the 1930 Walker Cup match at Royal St George's.*

holes and returned a 75 while Macdonald Smith came storming after him to finish second, two strokes behind, with a 70.

With three down and just one to go, many felt he had the hardest events under his belt and that the US Amateur at Merion would be the easiest of the four championships for Jones. However, having to beat five top amateurs within the space of four days is never easy. But Jones had the advantage of playing at Merion, one of his favorite courses. It held a special place in Jones' heart for it was at Merion that he had competed in his first Amateur title as a 14-year-old in 1916, and it was over the Pennsylvania course that he had won his first title in 1924.

The fans flocked to the course in numbers never before seen at the championship as public interest in one tournament was at its highest since the day Francis Ouimet had clinched the Open in 1913. They saw Jones first beat two Canadians, C. Ross Somerville 5 & 4 and then F.G. Hoblitzel, also 5 & 4. In the third round he beat Fay Coleman 6 & 5 and another easy victory followed in the semi-final when Jones beat Jess Sweetser 9 & 8. Even Jones could not have expected his passage to the final

1913 US OPEN FINAL SCORES

Score	Player	Country	Rounds
304	Francis Ouimet	(USA-Amateur)	77-74-74-79
304	Harry Vardon	(GB)	75-72-78-79
304	Ted Ray	(GB)	79-70-76-79
307	Walter Hagen	(USA)	73-78-76-80
307	Louis Tellier	(France)	76-76-79-76
307	Jim Barnes	(USA)	74-76-78-79
307	Macdonald Smith	(USA)	71-79-80-77

PLAY-OFF SCORES

	1	2	3	4	5	6	7	8	9	Out	10	11	12	13	14	15	16	17	18	In	Total
OUIMET	5	4	4	4	5	4	4	3	5	38	3	4	4	4	5	4	3	3	4	34	72
VARDON	5	4	4	4	5	3	4	4	5	38	4	4	5	3	5	4	3	5	6	39	77
RAY	5	4	5	4	5	4	3	3	5	38	4	4	5	4	5	6	4	5	3	40	78

HAGEN & JONES' DOMINATION

1914 Hagen: US Open
1919 Hagen: US Open
1921 Hagen: US PGA
1922 Hagen: British Open
1923 Jones: US Open
1924 Hagen: British Open, US PGA
Jones: US Amateur
1925 Hagen: US PGA
Jones: US Amateur
1926 Hagen: US PGA
Jones: US Open, British Open
1927 Hagen: US PGA
Jones: British Open, US Amateur
1928 Hagen: British Open
Jones: US Amateur
1929 Hagen: British Open
Jones: US Open
1930 Jones: US Open, British Open, US Amateur, British Amateur

Below: *Jones (left) and Hagen dominated the golf world throughout the 1920s. They are seen here during the 1934 Masters, one of Jones' few competitive appearances after 1930.*

Above: *Bobby Jones driving off on the opening day of the new Bobby Jones Municipal Course in Atlanta, Georgia.*

Right: *The provost of St Andrews, R. Leonard, presents Bobby Jones with the Freedom of the Burgh in 1958.*

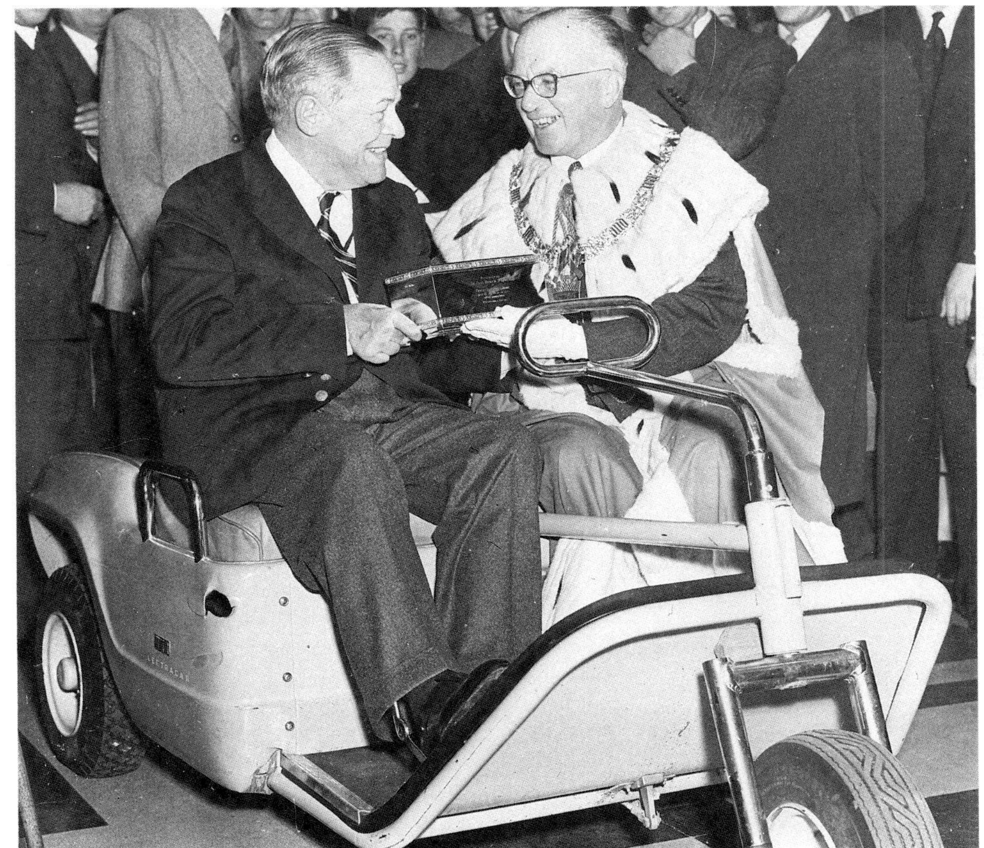

to be as easy as it had been. Only Eugene Homans stood between Jones and the Grand Slam and, like the others before him, could provide little opposition as Jones went on to complete golf's greatest ever achievement with an 8 & 7 win.

Jones announced his retirement from competitive golf shortly after to concentrate on his law practice. He was only 28 at the time but, in 10 years, along with Walter Hagen, he had helped establish American golfers as the greatest in the world. And, as the 1930s approached, the burden of carrying on where Hagen and Jones had left off fell upon the shoulders of the likes of Gene Sarazen and Tommy Armour. They did the job capably until the arrival of the next Golden Era of American golf with the coming of Nelson, Snead and Hogan.

NELSON, SNEAD AND HOGAN'S DOMINATION

In the ten years between 1945 and 1954 three men dominated the American golf scene. The invincible trio consisted of one Virginian, Sam Snead, and two Texans, Byron Nelson and Ben Hogan. Between them they won 14 majors in the United States during that period plus another five won before or during the war.

Nelson went into partial retirement as the 1950s approached and it was left to Hogan and Snead to become central characters in the golf world as they dominated the Masters, US Open and PGA Championship. Nelson lost a large part of his career because of the war but his contribution towards the trio's great achievements is there for all to see today. Nelson shattered PGA records by winning 18 tournaments in one year, including 11 in succession. Those feats are likely to remain in the record books for a long time – if not for ever.

It is with that amazing record that we begin an in-depth look at the ten-year domination of these three great golfers.

Sam Snead

Byron Nelson

Ben Hogan

NELSON'S TOUR RECORD

John Byron Nelson, Junior was born at Fort Worth, Texas in 1912. He worked as a caddie for a time before he turned professional in 1933. Four years later, in 1937, he beat Ralph Guldahl, by making up six strokes in two holes, to win his first Masters title and he also gained the first of his Ryder Cup selections that year. Two years after his Masters success, Nelson was US Open champion when he beat Craig Wood and Denny Shute in a play-off. Wood took him to the second extra 18 holes before Nelson won by three strokes.

Sadly, the war years coincided with Nelson's rise to the top but in 1942 he won the last Masters before the tournament was abandoned during the hostilities. It was a memorable win over his great contemporary Hogan. In an epic play-off he built up a six-stroke lead before eventually winning by just one stroke after an amazing comeback by Hogan.

In 1944 Nelson entered 23 tourna-

Right: *Byron Nelson in 1937, the year of his first major win, the Masters.*

Far right: *That swing and style was to carry Nelson to a staggering 18 wins in the 1945 season.*

BYRON NELSON'S YEAR (1945)

Nelson's run of 11 straight victories was as follows:

11 Mar MIAMI FOUR-BALL (with Jug McSpaden),
Miami Springs Course, Miami, Florida

20 Mar CHARLOTTE OPEN,
Myers Park GC, Charlotte, North Carolina

25 Mar GREENSBORO OPEN,
Starmount CC, Greensboro, North Carolina

1 Apr DURHAM OPEN,
Hope Valley CC, Durham, North Carolina

8 Apr ATLANTA OPEN,
Capital City Course, Atlanta, Georgia

10 Jun MONTREAL OPEN,
Islemere Golf & Country Club, Montreal, Canada

17 Jun PHILADELPHIA INQUIRER INVITATIONAL,
Llanerch CC, Philadelphia, Pennsylvania

1 Jul CHICAGO VICTORY NATIONAL OPEN,
Calumet CC, Chicago, Illinois

15 Jul PGA CHAMPIONSHIP,
Morraine CC, Dayton, Ohio

29 Jul TAM O'SHANTER OPEN,
Tam O'Shanter CC, Chicago, Illinois

4 Aug CANADIAN OPEN,
Thornhill CC, Toronto, Canada

Above, left: *Ralph Guldahl won the 1937 Open but Nelson made up six strokes in two holes to beat him in the 1937 Masters.*

Above: *Craig Wood, pictured after his 1941 Open victory, and Denny Shute lost to Nelson in a play-off for the 1939 US Open.*

ments and won 11 of them. Eight of these were on the US Tour and this created a new Tour record beating Sam Snead's tally of seven set in 1938. Nelson also created a new money-winning record with $37,967, paid in War Bonds.

Nelson's greatest year was to be 1945. Not only did he win the PGA title for the second time but he shattered all Tour records with 18 wins from 31 tournaments, including 11 consecutive successes. His stroke average for the season was 68.33 and, at one stage during the season, he put together 19 successive rounds under 70. Once more he shattered the prize money record with $63,335, and in winning the Seattle Open his four-round total of 259 was a new tournament record that stood until Mike Souchak lowered it by two in 1955.

The amazing run of success started in the Phoenix Open on 14 January when Nelson beat Denny Shute by two strokes to take the title.

His fourth win of the season was in the Miami Four Ball at Miami Springs on 11 March when Nelson and partner, Jug McSpaden, beat Sam Byrd and Denny Shute 8 & 6. That victory heralded the start of the astonishing 11-tournament-winning sequence which included a 4 & 3 victory in the final of the PGA title at Morraine, Ohio. The sequence stretched to 4 August when Nelson won the Canadian Open at Thornhill Country Club, Toronto. His next tournament was the Memphis Open two weeks later and he finished joint fourth behind winner Fred Haas junior. He returned to winning ways in the Knoxville Invitational the following week and went on to win three more tournaments before the year was out to shatter his own US Tour record of eight wins in one calendar year.

Some cynics suggested that Nelson would not have amassed his records had other top golfers not been on active service (Nelson was exempt from military service because he was a haemophiliac), or if the PGA had not relaxed some of its rules, notably the one concerning preferred lies. But Sam Snead was on the Tour that year and dominated it in the early part of the season, leading Nelson in tournament wins at one stage. When Nelson started his run of 11 straight wins it ended a run of three straight successes by Snead who had won six tournaments during the season. To dominate 'Slammin' Sam' the way he did was an achievement in its own right.

Those cynics were unkind. Nelson's record was a magnificent achievement by any standards and one that a present day golfer is unlikely to match.

The nearest any golfer has come to matching Nelson was 1946 when Hogan won 13. Hogan also notched up 11 wins in 1948 and Snead had ten in 1950. These are the only occasions double figures have been reached which highlights the magnitude of Nelson's performance.

Below: *Nelson on his way to one of his 1945 victories, in the Canadian Open.*

THE RYDER CUP RESUMES

Naturally, Hogan, Nelson and Snead were among the first names pencilled in when the United States team was announced for the 1947 Ryder Cup match, the first for ten years.

The match, however, nearly did not take place as the British were haggling over the dates. They wanted it at the end of their season in either late November or December while the Americans wanted a September date. During the 1947 British Open at Hoylake, R.C.T. Roe, secretary of the British PGA, announced that the 1947 event would not take place because a suitable date could not be agreed upon.

However, the on-off saga ended in August when the British agreed to come to the States on 1/2 November, thanks largely to the benevolence of Portland businessman Robert Hudson who agreed to finance part of the British team's stay. Portland, Oregon, was chosen as the venue for the first match since 1937 when Walter Hagen had led the American team to an 8-4 victory over Charles Whitcombe's team at the Southport & Ainsdale Club on the Lancashire coast.

Hagen, who had captained the United States team in all six previous Ryder Cup matches, was chosen as a non-playing co-captain with Craig Wood, who had been chosen as captain for the postponed match in 1941. The home team also appointed a playing captain, and that honor went to Ben Hogan.

Henry Cotton was the playing captain of the Great Britain team and he and his nine playing colleagues arrived at New York on 23 October. At a reception at the Waldorf Hotel that evening he said in an inteview that he was confident of taking the trophy back home with him.

Although the British were trailing 4-2 in the series, they arrived with one of their best ever teams. Cotton, Welshman Dai Rees and Charlie Ward had all had experience of playing in the United States before and Rees, Cotton and Sam King were survivors from the Southport match. On that occasion Rees had had a magnificent 3 & 1 win over Byron Nelson in the singles.

While the British team was one of their best ever the American team was even better and was littered with talent. Nelson, Hogan and Snead had won eight majors between them. Lloyd Mangrum and Herman Keiser were also former 'major' winners, and they were joined by the reigning Open and Masters champions, Lew Worsham and Jimmy Demaret. The British team, however, was undaunted by the impressive record of their counterparts and Irishman Fred Daly, the reigning British Open champion, joking as always said: 'The trophy's already on the ship . . .'.

The three giants of American golf in the immediate post-war era, Ben Hogan (left), Byron Nelson (center) and Sam Snead.

The larger American ball was to be used and this gave an obvious advantage to the home team. But, at the end of two days play, it made little difference what was used, the British would never have won.

A crowd of 3500 gathered on the opening morning and they basked in glorious sunshine. At the end of the morning 18 holes of the foursomes they had been treated to top class golf and the match stood level with each side ahead in two pairings. Lew Worsham and Porky Oliver were well up on Cotton and Arthur Lees, and Snead and Mangrum were on their way to a big win over Daly and Ward. The British saviors were Max Faulkner and James Adams who were leading Hogan and Demaret, while Nelson and Herman Barron were trailing Rees and King.

A downpour in the afternoon changed conditions dramatically. October had been the wettest in the area for 65 years and this latest soaking did not help playing conditions. A lot of casual water could be found on the greens, fairways, and in the bunkers. Conditions under foot were marshy. Many felt this would suit the British but it helped the home players more.

Above: *Henry Cotton (left) and Lloyd Mangrum, captains of the opposing 1953 Ryder Cup teams. Britain fared better then than they did under Cotton's captaincy in 1947, losing by one point.*

Left: *Sam Snead practicing for the 1953 Ryder Cup.*

Worsham and Oliver continued their massacre of Cotton and Lees by winning 10 & 9, to equal the foursomes record of Walter Hagen and Densmore Shute over George Duncan and Archie Havers in 1931. Snead and Mangrum beat Daly and Ward 6 & 5 . . . perhaps Daly was then sent to recover the trophy from the ship! The first day

Below: *American captain Ben Hogan, who left himself out of the second day's singles in the 1947 Ryder Cup match. His team did quite well without him . . . winning 11-1!*

whitewash was completed with two great recoveries. Nelson and Barron were trailing Rees and King until the 29th when Nelson dropped a 15-foot putt to level the match. The Americans won the next two holes and held on for a 2 & 1 victory. Faulkner and Adams, who had looked the best British pair in the morning, were four up after nine holes, and still two up at the half-way stage. Hogan and Demaret picked up four holes in the first seven holes of the afternoon session, taking the lead for the first time at the 25th hole. The Britons levelled it again at the 33rd but the home pair went ahead at the next hole, the 34th, and then clinched the match by taking the 36th to win by two.

The downpour in the afternoon left conditions so bad that it was hard to imagine good golf being played, but there was some. On the other hand, there was some dreadful golf – mostly played by the visitors.

In five of the six previous Ryder Cup matches the Great Britain team had trailed at the end of the foursomes but never before had they failed to score. They now went into the second day's singles facing a monumental task. Henry Cotton, perhaps surprisingly, stuck to the same British team for the singles, which meant Reg Horne and Eric Green made the journey to the USA without getting a game. Ben Hogan, however, left himself and Barron out, sending out replacements Dutch Harrison and Herman Keiser.

The morning session ended in much the same vein as the foursomes with the home team leading in six matches with one match level. Dai Rees was the only British hope, leading Jimmy Demaret.

An American victory was not in doubt but the question being asked by the gallery was: 'Could this be the first complete whitewash in the Cup's history?' The way the British team was playing, there was every chance.

Throughout the afternoon rain pelted down on the players and the small number of brave fans who turned out. Nonetheless the Americans returned to the clubhouse one after the other with big wins under their belts. Dutch Harrison beat Fred Daly 5 & 4. Mangrum beat Faulkner 6 & 5, Oliver beat Ward 4 & 3 and Henry Cotton, the

1947 RYDER CUP

FOURSOMES
(US names first)

E. Oliver & L. Worsham beat
H. Cotton & A. Lees 10 & 9

L. Mangrum & S. Snead beat
F. Daly & C. Ward 6 & 5

J. Demaret & B. Hogan beat
J. Adams & M. Faulkner 2 holes

H. Barron & B. Nelson beat
D. Rees & S. King 2 & 1

SINGLES

E. Harrison	beat	F. Daly	5 & 4
L. Worsham	beat	J. Adams	3 & 2
L. Mangrum	beat	M. Faulkner	6 & 5
E. Oliver	beat	C. Ward	4 & 3
B. Nelson	beat	A. Lees	2 & 1
S. Snead	beat	H. Cotton	5 & 4
J. Demaret	beat	D. Rees	3 & 2
H. Keiser	lost to	S. King	4 & 3

British captain, suffered his second big defeat when losing 5 & 4 to Sam Snead. Cotton, accompanied by his wife, did not enjoy his day, and was edgy and unsettled. A confrontation with a cameraman resulted in him refusing to play a shot until the cameraman was removed from the area. When he did resume, Cotton hit his ball into a tree. The Englishman was two up after the first nine holes but then lost four of the first five of the second nine in the morning. Nevertheless he pulled back to be just one down going into the final nine holes, and once more he lost four of the first five. That sealed a miserable Ryder Cup for the visiting captain.

Lew Worsham and Byron Nelson both contributed towards the impending 'whitewash' with wins over Adams and Lees. And just as Dai Rees looked like putting Britain's first points on the scoreboard, he threw away a one hole advantage with eight to play by losing the 29th, 30th, 31st and 32nd holes. Demaret went on to win 3 & 2. That only left mild-mannered Sam King who managed to beat Herman Keiser 4 & 3.

The Americans won the cup to take a 5-2 lead in the series in the most one-sided match ever, beating their 9-3 wins at Columbus, Ohio, in 1931 and at Ridgewood, New Jersey four years later. The Britons had arrived with such confidence, backed by one of their strongest teams ever. But how ironic it was they should play some of the worst golf seen in the Cup.

The defeat marked the end of one of the blackest years in British golf in which the Americans had strengthened their stranglehold by winning both the Ryder Cup and Walker Cup, and providing both the mens' and womens' winners of the British amateur championships with William Turnesa and Babe Zaharias. Amateur Frank Stranahan also came close to winning the British Open when he finished joint second, just one stroke behind the winner Fred Daly.

Ben Hogan can proudly say he led one of the best American Ryder Cup teams but the following year it was back to winning personal honors for the likable Texan when he went on to win the US Open and PGA titles. But if 1948 belonged to Hogan then 1949 belonged to Sam Snead.

Left: *Hogan (right) and Snead seen here during the 1956 Canada Cup (now World Cup) which they won for the United States.*

Below: *Byron Nelson (left) went on to become the non-playing American Ryder Cup captain in 1965. He is seen with his opposite number, Harry Weetman.*

SNEAD'S FIRST MASTERS

With Hogan being sidelined following his dreadful car accident near El Paso in February 1949, Snead was left with center stage all to himself and he took full advantage by winning the PGA title at Richmond and the Masters at Augusta. He also finished joint second in the US Open.

Snead, like Nelson and Hogan, was born in 1912. He turned professional in 1933. Prior to 1949 his career had been one of near misses and bad luck. His only major championship had been the 1942 PGA, although he had been in contention for many other titles – including the 1939 Open at Philadelphia when he took an eight at the final hole when a par five would have given him a Championship that in fact he was never to win.

But the 1949 Masters saw him produce two of the finest finishing rounds ever seen in the tournament and his two 67s were the best finish until bettered by Jack Nicklaus with a 64 and 69 in 1965. Awful weather threatened the tournament and two days before the start, on 7 April, the course was closed because of waterlogging. The conditions were so bad, that on the final day's practice only one man, the 1935 winner Gene Sarazen, had a sub-

Above: *Two final rounds of 67-67 assured Sam Snead of his first Masters title in 1949. The ability to play difficult shots like this was one of the qualities which made Snead a great player.*

1949 MASTERS Final positions	
282 Sam Snead	73-75-67-67
285 Johnny Bulla	74-73-69-69
285 Lloyd Mangrum	69-74-72-70
286 Johnny Palmer	73-71-70-72
286 Jim Turnesa	73-72-71-70
289 Lew Worsham	76-75-70-68

par round. Sarazen was one of eight former winners in the field, including the first winner Horton Smith. Ralph Guldahl, the 1939 winner, was the only former champion missing.

The favorites for the title were Byron Nelson, who had been in Augusta practicing for two weeks, Memphis dentist Cary Middlecoff, who was second in the money list to Lloyd Mangrum, and Mangrum himself. Snead, of course, could never be ignored as he was rarely far away from the leading bunch.

Despite the rain the putting surfaces at Augusta were still hard and fast. The rain did, however, have its advantages. The dogwood and azaleas that lined the fairways were in full bloom and the evergreen was fresh, making the setting as beautiful as ever.

Fifty-eight invited players teed off for the 13th Masters, including defending champion Claude Harmon who was attempting to become the first man to win back-to-back titles. Strong winds affected most players on the first day – except Lloyd Mangrum who putted brilliantly to return an opening round of 69 just as he had done a year earlier. Mangrum, holder of the Masters record 64 in 1940, was superb on the putting surface, one-putting on six greens. He even had the audacity to chip in from the bunker at the par-four 7th. Amateur Frank Stranahan pushed Mangrum all the way with a 70, despite a six at the 2nd. Middlecoff, installed as the tournament favorite just before the start, returned a 76 while Snead opened his account with a one-over par 73.

Strong winds on the second day resulted in high scoring again and only five men broke par, one less than on the first day. Snead shot a 75 to tie 14th place four over par for the tournament. The hero of the second day, however, was Ryder Cup player Herman Keiser who shared the lead with Mangrum on 143 with a tournament best 68. Keiser, who beat Hogan by one stroke to win the title in 1946, played methodically to beat the bad conditions. He served notice of his intentions with a magnificent birdie putt from 30 feet at the first hole. Amateur Stranahan was still up with the leaders until putting his ball in the pond at the 12th. Mangrum returned a 74 as a result of missing the greens with many of his second shots and the favorite Middlecoff bid his chances farewell when he added a 77 to his first round 76 to go nine over.

The 'best-dresser' award went, as usual, to Jimmy Demaret. Renowned for his flamboyant attire, he was seen wearing a blue shirt, cream trousers with a red belt, yellow socks, and his familiar green suede shoes!

The proceedings certainly heated up on the third day – in more ways than one. Gone were the strong winds – there was the welcome sight of the hot sun which brought the crowds out at last. The action on the course was getting pretty hot as well as only two strokes separated the first seven players.

Sam Snead made his move with a great 67 after going out in 32, four under par. His playing partner was Johnny Palmer, who took the undisputed lead on 214 thanks to a 70, his

Below: *Sam Snead (left) and Jim Turnesa hold the PGA trophy before the 1942 Final. Snead won 2 & 1.*

second successive round below par. The 30-year-old Palmer, from North Carolina, was enjoying his greatest moment in golf. A former B-29 gunner with a fine war record, he was hoping to start building an equally impressive golf record. Playing with Snead undoubtedly helped Palmer to raise his game to new heights.

Lloyd Mangrum was in the chasing group, as was Snead and Hollywood actor Joe Kirkwood, Junior, son of the famous trick-shot expert. The overnight joint leader Herman Keiser could not recover after a five at the 1st and an eight at the 2nd, and ended up on 78 and completely out of contention.

One of the largest galleries ever seen at Augusta, in the region of 15,000, came to witness one of the Masters great finishing rounds. Palmer slipped away from the lead with a par 72 after a six at the 8th when he hit a tree, and a five at the par-three 12th. Mangrum stayed near the front, as he had done from the start, and was joined in a tie for second place by the former commercial airline pilot Johnny Bulla who stormed through with a second successive 69. Kirkwood dropped out of the limelight completely after a disastrous final round. But the day belonged to one man, Sam Snead.

Left: *The classic swing of 'Slammin' Sam' Snead that became his trademark.*

Below: *Snead displaying the unorthodox 'sidewinder' putting style that he adopted in later years.*

Quite often in the past Snead's short putting game had let him down, particularly in big events. On this occasion that was all behind him, and his putting was one of the better features of his play.

Snead played with Jim Turnesa and enjoyed a one-stroke advantage over the New Yorker at the start of the day. Snead birdied the first hole from 20 feet and birdied the next. Turnesa pulled back slightly but Snead still led by two at the halfway stage. But then, at the 10th and 11th, Snead had two 5s to Turnesa's two pars. They were level – but not for long. At the 12th Turnesa found the water for a five while Snead was down for a birdie two. Snead went from strength to strength and got birdies at 13 and 15 before sinking an 18-foot birdie putt at the 18th to complete his second successive round of 67.

Snead was a popular winner and he had to thank his putter for his success – for a change. He had changed his putting style just before the Greensboro Open, which he won. The new style worked for him then, and it worked for him at Augusta.

No man had won the Masters in successive years. Many had tried, some had come close, some not so close. Sam Snead was attempting to make history in 1950 when he returned to the magnificent Augusta course.

JIMMY DEMARET UPSTAGES HOGAN AND SNEAD

Snead had been suffering from back trouble leading up to the tournament, but had been playing well, and was in with a chance of winning the event back-to-back. Hogan, playing his first 'major' since his car accident said he had never felt better. But Snead was the top money winner, reigning PGA champion and defending Masters champion. He had the right credentials to win the title a second time.

Naturally all eyes were on Ben Hogan. It was his first big test since his accident. He made his comeback three months earlier in the Los Angeles Open, but this was the real test. If his practice rounds of 67 and 68 were anything to go by – he was ready for it.

While the field of 65, including 13 amateurs, was littered with household names, the first day leader was the little-known Skee Riegel. A new professional, the former national amateur champion and Walker Cup player was helped by a series of successful long putts as he overcame the windy conditions. Five players were just one stroke behind Riegel on 70, including Jimmy Demaret and Horton Smith, both former Masters champions. Defending champion Snead kept an eye on proceedings with a 71 and Hogan, whose round with Australian Norman Von Nida attracted the biggest gallery, showed his old form apart from a couple of bogeys to return a 73.

Former PGA champion Jim Ferrier built up a four-stroke lead on the second day with a perfect round of 67 as Riegel slipped down the leader board. Ferrier's only challenge came from Ben Hogan who was being encouraged by the large crowd. Hogan returned a 68. Ferrier was playing an hour behind the Texan and was fully aware of his charge. A 197-pound ex-rugby player from Australia, Ferrier responded magnificently with three birdies in the opening nine holes. By contrast to the first day when cold winds prevailed, it was now warm and calm but it was not one of Sam Snead's better days and he came home with a 74 which included five 5s and a 6.

Ferrier held on to his lead at the end of round three but Hogan continued to breathe down his neck and pulled back two strokes. With Hogan in such form how could one bet against him winning his first Masters?

It was only in the second nine holes that Hogan had started to pick away at Ferrier's lead. Once Ferrier was in the club house with his 73 posted, Hogan

Above: *The flamboyantly dressed Jimmy Demaret, who won the 1950 Masters with a final round of 67.*

Right: *Hogan (driving) and Snead threw away their chances of the 1950 Masters after final rounds of 76 and 72.*

then attacked. As dusk approached, 10,000 fans were still on the course as Hogan approached the 18th. He was one behind Ferrier and had a 20-foot putt for a birdie to go into the final round all square. The ball rolled past the hole by three feet. He missed the return for a five and a two-stroke deficit, much to the crowd's disappointment.

Byron Nelson had one of the best rounds of the day, a 69 to tie him in third place with Jimmy Demaret, four behind the leader. But spare a thought for Ryder Cup player Herman Barron who took an 11 at the par-three 16th after putting three balls in the water!

Eighteen thousand fans filled the course on the final day. Many of them had come to see a Ben Hogan victory. What they did witness over the last 18

Above: *Byron Nelson who shot a great 69 in the third round at Augusta.*

Right: *Jimmy Demaret (center) looks elated after receiving a plaque from Bobby Jones to commemorate his great win.*

Far right: *If the drive is not stylish, Jimmy Demaret's clothes certainly are!*

holes was beyond their wildest belief. The overnight leaderboard was thrown into total disruption. Hogan was two over after five holes, and his chance of glory seemed gone. Snead was making his charge with a 72 but it was too late for him to retain the title. Nelson had a two over par 74 and that left just two men – Ferrier and Demaret.

Demaret had been delighting the crowds with his colorful clothing all week. Now he was to delight them with his golf as well. The last day of the tournament was Easter Sunday and Demaret dressed in an all-green outfit for the occasion. He started the final round four strokes behind Ferrier and promptly dropped another shot with a five at the first, but that was his only bogey in the first nine. Ferrier, who was playing in the last group on the course, went out in 34, thus gaining another shot. However, Demaret birdied the 10th and 13th before bogeying 14, but he came back with two more birdies in succession to set up an inward nine of 34.

Ferrier was aware of the situation ahead of him. He led by five with nine to play – how could he lose? But lose he did. He dropped five strokes on the last six holes including a demoralizing three putt on the 18th. He hung on for second place but Jimmy Demaret committed one of the biggest acts of larceny in Masters history.

The flamboyant Texan picked up the winners cheque for $2400 and when presented with it by Bobby Jones, he took the microphone and sang 'How Lucky You Are?' . . . how true!

Many of the thousands who flocked to Georgia were there to see a Ben Hogan victory. That would have beaten all fairy tales if he had come back from his atrocious injuries in that car accident. His next chance to write his own piece of golfing history came two months later at Merion, Pennsylvania when he challenged for the US Open.

1950 US MASTERS

Final positions

283 Jimmy Demaret	70-72-72-69
285 Jim Ferrier	70-67-73-75
287 Sam Snead	71-74-70-72
288 Ben Hogan	73-68-71-76
288 Byron Nelson	75-70-69-74

Ferrier v Demaret: Hole-by-hole finish over the final 18

Ferrier	4 4 5 3 4 2 3 5 4 (34)	
	4 4 3 6 5 5 4 5 5 (41)	75
Demaret	5 5 4 3 4 3 4 4 3 (35)	
	4 4 3 4 5 4 2 4 4 (34)	69

Hogan's Open Win on a Tide of Emotion

Unlike the Masters, Hogan had won the Open before, in 1948. Only his accident prevented him from defending the title. Now he was ready to win his second title. The legs, which many felt would not stand up to the pace, proved themselves to be in perfect working order in the Masters. The only difference this time was that the final day consisted of two rounds – would his legs be able to withstand that treatment? Hogan's biggest challenge was expected to come from his great rival Sam Snead, who had swept the honors during Hogan's year of enforced retirement.

While all eyes were on the big two, a little-known professional from Alabama, Lee Mackey Junior swept through the field on the first day to enjoy his one moment of glory in the game. His 64 created a new Open record, beating Jimmy McHale's old record by one. But, as often happens, such moments of sheer magic have the habit of turning sour. They did just that for Mackey and Al Bosch, who finished second to Mackey on the opening day with a 67. On day two they both returned scores 17 strokes worse than their first round totals. Bosch failed to make the cut.

Although Mackey picked up a larger gallery on the second day, Hogan was still the star attraction. How the American fans would love him to win. They shared his heartache at the time of his accident. They admired his courage in saving his wife from the impact of the crash and they wanted such bravery rewarded with a win at Merion. His second round 69 was good enough to bring him up among the leaders on 141 as Dutch Harrison took the overall lead with a 67 for a 139. Hogan now faced his biggest test since

Above: *Hogan on his way to winning the 1953 British Open at Carnoustie, just one of his three major titles that year.*

Left: *Ben Hogan, the central character in one of sport's great fairytales.*

his comeback at Los Angeles in January – two gruelling rounds, in the world's toughest competition, in one day.

The legs stood up to it alright, but three disastrous holes cost him an outright win on the Saturday.

Attendance records were broken as 15,000-plus turned up at the famous

1950 US OPEN

Final positions:

287 George Fazio	73-72-72-70
287 Ben Hogan	72-69-72-74
287 Lloyd Mangrum	72-70-69-76
288 Dutch Harrison	72-67-73-76
289 Jim Ferrier	71-69-74-75
289 Joe Kirkwood Jnr	71-74-74-70
289 Henry Ransom	72-71-73-73

Play-off scores, hole-by-hole

Hogan	4 5 3 5 4 4 3 5 3 (36)	4 4 4 3 4 4 4 2 4 (33)	69
Mangrum	4 4 4 5 4 4 4 4 3 (36)	5 3 5 3 5 3 6 3 4 (37)	73
Fazio	5 4 3 5 4 5 5 3 3 (37)	4 4 4 3 5 5 5 3 5 (38)	75

great recovery shot to within six feet of the pin. But, although his putt was on line it finished short. All of a sudden panic buttons started flashing. Fortunately there was a halt in the decline as he parred the 18th to force an 18-hole play-off the following day.

Fazio was the least experienced of the three men in the play-off but at the half-way stage the 10,000 fans did not know who was the likely champion as the scores read: Hogan 36, Mangrum 36, Fazio 37. Then Fazio, the Pine Valley Club professional, tailed off during the second nine, leaving Mangrum and Hogan to do battle. First one then the other picked up a shot but, by the time they arrived at the 16th Hogan was one up. Then, in one moment of foolishness, Mangrum thoughtlessly picked up his ball from the putting surface to wipe away a fly that was resting on it. The action cost him a two-stroke penalty which meant Hogan led by three with two to play. He took full advantage with a birdie two at 17, before going on to win by four shots.

The thousands of fans at Merion, and millions more following Hogan's progress in the media, had waited for this moment since January. It had finally arrived. Ben Hogan had cheated death and overcome physical and mental barriers to carve his name into US Open golf history by winning one of the toughest ever championships. Only men of real character could have come through such an ordeal. Ben Hogan was that sort of man.

Above: *Despite his near-fatal accident, Ben Hogan lost none of his style.*

Below: *Lloyd Mangrum was the leader at the end of three rounds and then shot a 76.*

course, scene of so many great golfing moments in the past. Were they now going to witness another truly great moment?

At the end of the morning session Lloyd Mangrum was the new tournament leader, two strokes ahead of Hogan. But in the afternoon, as his rivals started faltering, Hogan played some of the most deliberate golf of his career. With his main rivals back in the club house he knew that Mangrum and George Fazio were in the lead level on 287. Hogan was two up on them going into the 15th. Pars all the way in would have given him his second title. But the 15th brought disaster.

After hitting the green in regulation two he three putted for a bogey five. He still led by one and, after making par at the 16th, he hit the green with his tee shot at the par three 17th only to see his ball roll into the bunker. He made a

HOGAN'S GREATEST-EVER PERFORMANCE

Hogan retained the US Open title in 1951 having also won that year's Masters. He was well and truly back and in 1953 he showed why he was the best golfer in the world by winning the Masters, US Open and British Open – a remarkable feat – to make him the only man to win three of the four major professional tournaments in one year. The first of those three championships saw, by Hogan's own admission, the best golf he ever played. It was breathtaking as he lowered the Masters record by five shots with rounds of 70-69-66-69, the first man to have three rounds under 70 in the history of the great tournament.

Conditions were ideal for record-breaking rounds. The weather was fine and the crowds poured in as they broke the first-day attendance record. Local storekeepers responded to the occasion by closing for the day for the first time on what they called 'Masters Day.' The course was in superb condition and all the past champions, except Herman Keiser and Ralph Guldahl, were among the record 73 invited competitors.

Left: *The champion-elect: Hogan walks through the large gallery at Carnoustie and (above) is presented with the British Open trophy in 1953.*

The practice sessions indicated records were in store as Julius Boros had a 67 and Ben Hogan, in good shape, had several sub par rounds, including a 66. But the preliminaries saw Lloyd Mangrum, the season's top money winner, emerge as favorite after he scored a blistering 63 which, had it been in tournament conditions, would have been an Augusta record.

It was not one of the big guns who was top of the leader board at the end of the first day but two-times PGA runner-up Chick Harbert with a 68. Harbert was the winner of the pre-Masters driving competition the day before the start of the championship. Hogan returned a 70 but would have joined Harbert had he not had bogeys at 17 and 18. Sam Snead also returned a 70, thanks to a monster 60-foot putt for a birdie three at the 18th. But it was

later realized that his playing partner, Byron Nelson, had marked him a four, which Snead had signed for. His score had, therefore, to be amended to a 71.

The remainder of the 1953 Masters was about one man – Ben Hogan.

He was out in 32 on the second day as he played some of the best golf of his illustrious career; he played the 4th, 5th and 6th holes in a total of eight strokes – two under par. Further birdies followed at the 8th and 9th, the latter being a stunner when his second shot, with an eight iron, at the 420-yard par four landed just three feet from the pin. He returned in 37 for a 69 and a tournament lead of one shot over Indiana gas-station owner Bob Hamilton, who also scored 69 on the day.

Hogan was, perhaps, a little fortunate to be in the afternoon group on day two because lightning and torrential rain caused morning play to be abandoned for half an hour. The rain made the greens more to Hogan's liking and he took full advantage of the 'Act of God.'

The greens, once more, were slightly slower and to Hogan's liking on the third day. Again he swept the opposition aside as he went out in another 32, completing the first nine holes with a 60-foot birdie putt. Hogan was playing with great keenness and enthusiasm, and came back in 34 for a 66 in his best ever round at Augusta. Hogan widened the gap at the top of the leader board with a new championship record 205 for 54 holes, beating Byron Nelson's 207. His nearest challenger was his playing partner Ed 'Porky' Oliver who tried to match the great man, and came in with a 67 for 209. Between them they had 13 birdies and one eagle and those statisticians among the crowd calculated their better ball score as a devastating 59. The key factor in Hogan's great round was his consistency and accuracy with his second shots. They were so good he only took 31 putts for the round, with just 14 on the first nine holes.

There was yet another storm on the fourth day followed by glorious sunshine and Hogan was again fortunate to play in the better of the weather. But it is hard to imagine him losing no matter what conditions he played in.

He started his final round with a birdie at the 2nd and again at the 3rd when he hit a three iron to within 10 inches of the hole. That set the pattern for his third consecutive round under 70 and he finished it with a birdie three at the 18th for a 69 and new Masters record total of 274, beating Ralph Guldahl and Claude Harmon's 279. Hogan's record stood until 1965 when beaten by the great Jack Nicklaus. Setting the Masters record completed a unique double for Hogan as he was also already the holder of the US Open record.

Ed Oliver was Hogan's nearest rival on 279, which equalled the old Masters record, but he was no match for Hogan who admitted afterwards that it was the best he had ever played over 72 holes. 'I hope to come back next year and play the same caliber of golf,' he added. 'If you do,' said his playing

Above: *Control of the club like this helped make Ben Hogan one of the greatest golfers of all time.*

Right: *Ben Hogan, winner of 62 US Tour events.*

1953 MASTERS

Leader board, round-by-round

Round One	Round Two	Round three	Final Scores
68 Chick Harbert	139 BEN HOGAN	205 BEN HOGAN	274 BEN HOGAN
69 Al Besselink	140 Bob Hamilton	209 Ed Oliver	279 Ed Oliver
69 Ed Oliver	141 Ted Kroll	211 Chick Harbert	282 Lloyd Mangrum
70 BEN HOGAN	141 Chick Harbert	213 Lloyd Mangrum	283 Bob Hamilton
70 Milon Marusic	142 Ed Oliver	214 Ted Kroll	285 Tommy Bolt
	142 Lloyd Mangrum	214 Al Beeselink	285 Chick Harbert
	142 Milon Marusic	214 Tommy Bolt	

partner Byron Nelson, 'you'll be on your own . . .'

Most professional sportsmen enjoy one of those days when everything goes right. Ben Hogan was lucky in April 1953 when he had four such days. The only hiccup being his two bogeys at the end of his first round.

After Hogan's two other 'majors' that season, the Nelson-Hogan-Snead era was nearly over. Sam Snead won the 1954 Masters and that turned out to be the last major success of the threesome. Snead went on to win a record 84 US Tour tournaments, Hogan 62 and Nelson 54 for a combined total of 200. Not even the next great 'Triumvirate' of Nicklaus, Palmer and Player could match that level of success.

THE SECOND GREAT TRIUMVIRATE PALMER-PLAYER-NICKLAUS

Just as the first Great Triumvirate of Braid, Taylor and Vardon dominated golf in the early part of the century so did Arnold Palmer, Gary Player and Jack Nicklaus during the 1960s and, to a certain extent, the 1970s.

Between them the Big Three, as they became known, won 34 'Majors' including at least one a year every year between 1958 and 1975 (with the exception of 1969). Their great run of success was started by Palmer when he won the 1958 Masters and Player continued the run by winning the British Open a year later. The following year Palmer won one of the truly remarkable tournaments when he came from seven behind third-round leader Mike Souchak in the US Open to snatch a two-stroke victory from an up-and-coming young amateur – Jack Nicklaus.

Arnold Palmer

Gary Player

Jack Nicklaus

PALMER'S GREAT RECOVERY

Palmer's remarkable comeback in one of his now legendary 'charges' was in the first Open for 22 years to be held on the Cherry Hills, Denver, course. He went into the tournament as clear favorite after a great season up to the Open in which he had won the Masters as well as the Insurance City Tournament, Palm Springs Classic, Baton Rouge Tournament and Pensacola Open. He was having his best season ever, and was confident of adding his first Open to his impressive list of titles.

However, he ended the first day at Cherry Hills well down the leader board and was four shots behind pacesetter Mike Souchak. Palmer could well have been further in arrears had it not been for an unsuspecting youngster who removed Palmer's ball from the creek alongside the first hole, which resulted in him dropping for a one-stroke penalty when he could easily have taken more strokes attempting to get out of the creek using his own resources.

At the half-way stage Palmer had slipped further behind Souchak who added a 67 to his first day 68 for an outstanding two-round total of 135. Palmer had a 71 for 143 and talk of victory for the man from Latrobe, Pennsylvania, was on very few lips. Few could see beyond Souchak as the eventual winner as he had built up a three-stroke lead over Doug Sanders at the end of his second round.

The third day consisted of 36 holes of golf and the final 18 provided one of the most amazing, and unbelievable finishes to any golf tournament, major or otherwise.

Souchak maintained his lead at the 54-hole mark but it had been cut to two shots, with Jerry Barber, Dow Finsterwald and Julius Boros in pursuit. The young Jack Nicklaus and the experienced, and much older, Ben Hogan were just one behind those three but Palmer was seven behind Souchak. Nicklaus was talked about as the likely winner at lunch, some even had a fancy for Hogan – what emotion that would have created – but only the brave were prepared to consider Palmer.

Palmer stood on the 55th tee full of confidence, despite his seven-stroke deficit. He knew he was capable of beating the course, which was playing fairly easy, and he also knew his opponents were capable of cracking up. His confidence was reflected right

1960 US OPEN

Scores after round three:
208 Mike Souchak
210 Dow Finsterwald
210 Julius Boros
210 Jerry Barber
211 Ben Hogan
211 Jack Nicklaus
215 ARNOLD PALMER

Scores after round four:
280 ARNOLD PALMER
282 Jack Nicklaus
283 Dutch Harrison
283 Julius Boros
283 Mike Souchak
283 Jack Fleck
283 Dow Finsterwald
283 Ted Kroll

Above: *Arnold Palmer followed up his memorable win at Cherry Hills in 1960 with the first of two successive British Open wins a year later.*

Right: *The determination on Palmer's face, and the dismay of his opponent, Gary Player, tell their own stories.*

from the start with four consecutive birdie threes as he blistered his way to an outward nine of 30, to equal Jimmy McHale's Open record set at St Louis in 1947. While Palmer had been picking up birdies and making regular pars, Souchak was letting it slip and by the time the New Yorker came to the tenth, with the others playing ahead of him, the young Nicklaus was the new leader, one ahead of Souchak and Jack Fleck, and two ahead of Hogan, Boros and Palmer. Souchak continued to

Above: *Palmer, for once without his 'army.'*

Right: *Arnold Palmer with a young, admiring, Peter Oosterhuis, during the 1971 Ryder Cup at St Louis, Missouri.*

Below: *Despite all the willing in the world, this putt from off the green stopped inches short of the hole. Nonetheless Palmer went on to win the tournament, the 1964 Masters.*

drop shots, as did Fleck but Palmer added three more birdies on the back nine for a round of 65 in the greatest finish ever seen in the Open, and his final total of 280 gave him a two-shot win over Nicklaus. The unfortunate and dejected Souchak ended up taking a six at the 72nd to deprive himself of the runners-up position.

Arnold Palmer had, at last, fulfilled his dream and become US Champion but even he, despite his oozing confidence, must have doubted, during the first 54 holes, that he was going to take the coveted title. Palmer's great recovery that day at Cherry Hills provided one of the most exciting finishes ever to a major tournament, and the famous 'Charge' of his was to become his trademark over the years but, while attempting to win his second Open in 1966, his good fortune deserted him and he had to endure the complete opposite of his Cherry Hills success when he *threw away* a seven-stroke lead before losing a play-off to Billy Casper.

PALMER'S REVERSAL

The scene of Palmer's *disaster* was the picturesque Californian course at the Olympic Country Club. It was not particularly long at 6727 yards but its vast quantity of trees, estimated at around 40,000, meant accurate driving was essential. That criterion certainly suited Palmer and the pre-tournament favorite, Jack Nicklaus, who, like Palmer, was looking for his second US Open title. Both, however, had to succumb to an unknown 37-year-old on the first day as Al Mengert from Tacoma shot an opening 67, four ahead of Palmer who had a disastrous opening nine holes with a 38.

Palmer shot a 66 on the second day, his best score in the Open since his great 65 which won him his first title six years earlier. He only missed one fairway and one green all day but, being the perfectionist he is, still found fault with his game. That ability to self-criticize is one of the things that has made Palmer a great champion over the years. His 66 gave him a share of the lead with Billy Casper who shot 68 to go with his first round 69.

On the third day Palmer started his 'charge' just as it seemed Casper was starting to get the upper hand. Palmer had at first pulled away from Casper but was surprised when the big Californian drew level at the 13th. It was then that Palmer 'changed gear' and birdied two of the last five to build up a three-stroke lead on 207. Perhaps surprisingly, it was the first time Palmer had ever led after 54 holes in the Open.

Nicklaus was just one behind Casper and a great finish was expected by the 15,000-plus fans as temperatures rose well into the eighties. The competition was just as hot. Palmer extended his lead over Casper who had pulled away from Nicklaus to become the only challenger.

Palmer shot a 32 on his outward nine while Casper shot 36. Palmer's lead was up to seven, with just nine to go, and he didn't even need his famous 'charge,' just a succession of steady golf shots would have sufficed. Casper picked up a shot at the 10th with a four to Palmer's five and he picked up another at the 13th with a three. They both made fours on the 14th but then it came to the par-three 15th, and the start of Palmer's disaster.

Still five up and with four to play, he needed four pars to break Ben Hogan's championship record of 276. He took a seven-iron but found the bunker. He got out to within eight feet, but two putted for a four while Casper made his birdie putt. Palmer now led by three, with three to play. Surely the great man would compose himself? He didn't; and further disaster followed.

Above: *Two young and up-and-coming golfers! Arnold Palmer (right) and a somewhat overweight Jack Nicklaus. The picture was taken in 1965.*

His drive at the 604-yard par-five hit a tree and went into the rough, just 180 yards from the teeing area. He took two shots to get out and then put his fourth into the sand once more. He got out in one and single putted but it was a six to Casper's birdie four. Suddenly, with two holes to go, Palmer's lead had been cut, in just two holes, from five to one. There was total disbelief around the packed course as history was repeating

itself for Palmer, but in reverse.

At the 17th his tee shot found the rough on the left, he squirted the ball out, but it found the rough on the right. He made the green with his next and then two putted while Casper made par. They were all level with one to play. Fortunately Palmer got a grip of himself and stopped the rot as both players made four to tie the tournament and force a play-off the next day.

Palmer had taken unnecessary chances at the 15th and 16th and they had cost him the title. At least he proved he was human and the play-off was to call for a super-human effort over another 18 holes as he had allowed the massive psychological advantage to slip away from him and swing towards Casper. How could he let it slip, particularly after the way he controlled himself, and his golf, to pull back those seven strokes at Cherry Hills six years earlier, remains a mystery to this day.

When the players resumed their duel, Palmer appeared to have matters under complete control and the 12,059 gallery had their confidence in Palmer restored as he built up a two-stroke lead after the first nine holes thanks to two birdies. After the previous day's second-nine disaster, it was unimaginable to think Palmer could fail again, but he went on to prove, what many did not believe, that he was really human.

Casper drew level at the par-four 11th with a birdie to Palmer's bogey and then, over four consecutive holes

Above, left: *Billy Casper trailed Palmer by two shots with eight to play in the play-off, but still won by four strokes.*

Above, right: *This birdie putt at the 14th in the final round could have helped to give Palmer the title.*

from the 13th, Casper picked up a stroke at each. Palmer pulled one back at the 17th but Casper birdied 18 for a 69 to Palmer's 73. Arnie's famous charge deserted him for the second day in succession as Casper went on to regain the title he first won at Winged Foot in 1959. The talk of Palmer throwing it away should not detract from Casper's play. He was one of the best putters around at the time, and it was that putting that saw him through the last day, and the subsequent play-off. He deserves a lot of the credit for his success, rather than accepting Palmer's disasters as the key to his victory.

Palmer never won the US Open title again after his 1960 success and he certainly never came as close again as he did at the Olympic Club in 1966 when his reversal went down as the biggest turnaround in US sport since the Chicago Cubs threw away an 8-0 lead after six innings to lose the 1929 World Series to the Philadelphia Athletics.

1966 US OPEN

Scores after 54 holes:	Scores after 63 holes:	Scores after 72 holes:
207 Arnold Palmer	239 Arnold Palmer	278 Billy Casper
210 Billy Casper	246 Billy Casper	278 Arnold Palmer
		285 Jack Nicklaus

Final Round scores:

	1	2	3	4	5	6	7	8	9	Out	10	11	12	13	14	15	16	17	18	In	Total
Par	5	4	3	4	4	4	4	3	4	35	4	4	4	3	4	3	5	4	4	35	70
Palmer	4	3	3	4	4	5	3	3	3	32	5	4	3	4	4	4	6	5	4	39	71
Casper	5	4	4	3	5	4	4	3	4	36	4	4	3	3	4	2	4	4	4	32	68

Play-off scores:

	1	2	3	4	5	6	7	8	9	Out	10	11	12	13	14	15	16	17	18	In	Total
Par	5	4	3	4	4	4	4	3	4	35	4	4	4	3	4	3	5	4	4	35	70
Palmer	5	4	3	3	4	4	3	3	4	33	4	5	4	3	5	4	7	4	4	40	73
Casper	5	4	3	4	5	4	3	2	5	35	4	3	4	2	4	3	6	5	3	34	69

THE GOLDEN BEAR ARRIVES

That play-off at the Olympic Club was the third contested by Palmer in the Open, and he lost all three. The previous one was when he and Jacky Cupit were soundly beaten by Julius Boros at Brookline in 1963 and the first occasion was a year earlier when a 22-year-old professional of just seven months beat him by three strokes. That youngster, without a professional win to his name at the time, was Jack Nicklaus, with whom Palmer was to share many memorable and exciting moments over the years.

The National Amateur champion in 1959 and 1961, Nicklaus served notice that he was going to be a player of the future when he pushed Palmer during his great win in the 1960 Open and then, a year later, while still an amateur, he finished joint fourth at Oakland Hills, behind winner Gene Littler. Of all players in the field for the 1962 championship at Oakmont, Pennsylvania, Nicklaus had the best two-year record, yet he had been an amateur in both years.

Played in Palmer's own back-yard, the record crowds that were to swamp the Oakmont course showed great partisanship for their own hero. The course was hosting its fourth Open. Tommy Armour had won in 1927, Sam Parks shot from obscurity to beat Walter Hagen and Gene Sarazen in 1935, and Ben Hogan won from Sam Snead in 1953. Hogan was the only winner to break par for his four-round total, but Palmer had every chance of emulating him as he knew this tough course inside-out, having played it more than 200 times.

Nicklaus came to Oakmont having

Jack Nicklaus, 1963-style.

come close to his first professional win the previous week when he finished second to Gene Littler, the defending Open champion, in the Thunderbird Classic at New Jersey. In 17 professional tournaments Nicklaus had never once been out of the money but he still had to win. He was young and confident and Palmer had a liking for the youngster. Knowing the course as he did, he felt it suited Nicklaus, who, because of his long-hitting, could hit his way 'over' trouble.

Rain cancelled the final day's practice, the first time there had been such a cancellation in the history of the Open, but the bad weather did not deter the crowds for the first day's play as 17,837

Left: *Nineteen-year-old Jack Nicklaus holding the winner's trophy after capturing the US Amateur title in 1959.*

Right: *Nicklaus on his way to winning his second US Amateur title, at Pebble Beach in 1961.*

Below: *Nicklaus blasting his way out of a bunker during the 1959 British Amateur championship at Sandwich.*

trod the course, the largest ever first-day gallery in the 62-year history of the Open – nearly 4000 more than the old record set at Cherry Hills two years earlier. The committee paired Nicklaus and Palmer together for the first 18 holes and when the youngster made birdie threes on the first three holes the gallery for their match was swelled even more. Nicklaus finished his round on 72, as a result of a seven on the par-five ninth. Palmer shot a 71 to be just two behind the first-day leader Littler.

Palmer was outstanding on the second day as he shot a 68 for a share of the lead on 139 with Bob Rosburg, runner-up in the 1959 Open to Billy Casper. Fog and slow play delayed proceedings but a new tournament record crowd of 19,971 delighted in Palmer's skills. Defending champion Littler faltered with a 74 while Nicklaus shot a 70 for a 142, but was still three behind Palmer.

Above: *Palmer 'socks it' to Nicklaus after the youngster had just beaten him in the play-off for the 1962 Open at Oakmont.*

Left: *Palmer can only watch as Nicklaus powers his way to the title, his first major tournament win.*

With the usual two rounds being completed on the third day the attendance record was shattered once more as a staggering 24,492 paid to witness the climax, many of them hoping to see Palmer's second win in three years.

Nicklaus gained a shot on Palmer after the morning 18 holes with a 72 and in the afternoon he gained two more to pull level then, at the 18th, both had chances to win the title outright. Nicklaus, playing ahead of Palmer, had his chance but the ball slipped past the cup. Then Palmer, too, missed his birdie putt and the 21st play-off in the Open was set up. It was the first play-off since 1957 when Dick Meyer beat Cary Middlecoff by seven strokes at the Inverness course.

A partisan 11,000 crowd turned up for the head-to-head confrontation, and they were stunned when 'their man' was trailing by four strokes after

Left: *Great concentration has made the Golden Bear one of the greatest golfers of all time.*

Above: *Defending champion Gene Littler could not contend with Palmer and Nicklaus in 1962.*

Below: *. . . nor could 1959 champion Billy Casper.*

1962 US OPEN

Final scores:
283 Jack Nicklaus
283 Arnold Palmer
(Nicklaus won play-off 71 to 74)
285 Phil Rodgers
285 Bobby Nichols
287 Gay Brewer
288 Gary Player
288 Tommy Jacobs

just six holes. Nicklaus increased his lead to five at the ninth but Palmer started a 'mini charge' when he pulled back two shots at the 11th and 12th. Nicklaus stayed cool and picked up another stroke at the 13th to give him a four-stroke lead with five to play. As Nicklaus stood on the verge of his first Open he must have been well aware how Palmer had won *his* first Open in 1960. But Nicklaus was in no mood to suffer the same fate as Mike Souchak and, as both players parred the next four holes it signalled the end of Palmer's absolute dominance and the birth of a new star.

Nicklaus won the tournament on the greens, only three-putting one of the 90 greens all week. He became the first Rookie to win the Open. Nicklaus certainly celebrated his first professional win in style and confirmed the beliefs of many who described him as another Bobby Jones after his first Amateur title in 1959. That indeed was a compliment but, as we now know, Nicklaus became as legendary as the great man himself. Palmer, in defeat, said: 'I'm sorry to say but he'll be around a long time.' As usual Arnie was right.

The subsequent record of Jack Nicklaus stands alone in the world of golf as he has gone on to win a total of 18 professional 'Majors,' more than any other man, and today he has proved he is still capable of winning the big tournaments.

Five shots behind Palmer and Nicklaus at Oakmont on that June day was the likable and friendly South African Gary Player who was to be the third member of golf's Big Three.

NICKLAUS'
MAJOR CHAMPIONSHIP
VICTORIES

1959 US Amateur
1961 US Amateur
1962 US Open
1963 Masters, PGA
1965 Masters
1966 British Open, Masters
1967 US Open
1970 British Open
1971 PGA
1972 US Open, Masters
1973 PGA
1975 Masters, PGA
1978 British Open
1980 US Open, PGA
1986 Masters

Jack Nicklaus demonstrates the tremendous power of his hitting in 1966, when he won his first British Open at Muirfield.

PLAYER – THE MATCH-PLAY KING

Player won the hearts of fans the world over with his generosity, warmth, good sportsmanship – and great skills. And his domination of the World Match-Play championship, played annually over England's Wentworth course, made him the best match-play golfer since Walter Hagen.

Player was invited to compete in the first tournament in 1964 but was crushed by eventual winner Arnold Palmer, 8 & 6, in the semi-final, after beating Ken Venturi in the opening round. But then, in the ten years from 1965 to 1974 Player started a domination of the event which saw him win the title a record five times from six final appearances.

In 1965 he won the US Open, joining Gene Sarazen and Ben Hogan as winners of all four 'Majors.' He also won the World Series of Golf and helped South Africa to their first World Cup. His play at Wentworth was his most impressive ever on an English course as he first beat 1964 runner-up Neil Coles 5 & 4, and then, in the semi-final, recovered from being seven down with 17 to play in one of the greatest come-backs since Palmer's recovery in the 1960 US Open.

Above: *Gary Player seen teeing off in 1956.*

Left: *Player not only won the World Match-Play title five times but the British Open three times. The first British Open success was in 1959.*

Playing Tony Lema, the South African lost seven of the last holes of the morning round to go into lunch six down. Lema won the first of the afternoon 18 holes but then Player turned in some of his finest golf to recover but was still two down with three to play. Lema lost the 34th and at the next sank an eight-footer but watched agonizedly as Player holed his five-footer to halve the hole. Somehow the small South African had to produce a win from the last hole. He hit a superb second shot wood to the heart of the green as Lema pulled his second.

Player made four and it was good enough to win the hole and halve the match. As twilight approached they went into the sudden-death play-off and Player, once more, hit a brilliant second shot with a wooden club to the heart of the green while Lema was short and bunkered, and it was all over. Player had won three of the last four holes to win one of the greatest matches seen in the championship, even to this day.

Player's opponent in the final was Australian Peter Thomson who beat Arnie Palmer in a 'no-love-lost' needle match semi-final. The final itself was

Right: *Player being presented with a 'replacement' trophy after beating Nicklaus in the 1966 World Match-Play Final. The original trophy had been mislaid.*

Below: *Player in action at Wentworth. His partner is Tony Lema and his caddie is the leading English cricketer, Ted Dexter.*

Above: *Being the best bunker-player in the world did not help Gary beat Arnold Palmer in the semi-final in 1964.*

Right: *Jack Nicklaus in action at Wentworth in 1966. Player beat him 6 & 4 in the final.*

not a great one, but was notable for its closeness as the South African went on to win 3 & 2 after both men played near-faultless golf.

He successfully defended his title with a 6 & 4 win over Jack Nicklaus in the following year's final after a tough tussle with Britain's Neil Coles in the first round. In his semi-final Player beat Palmer with a great display of how to use all the clubs in the bag. In the final he sustained his concentration as he beat his great friend, and intense rival, Jack Nicklaus. Nicklaus was surprisingly let down by his driving in the morning, and four bad drives cost him four holes. Despite playing great golf for the first 12 holes of the afternoon round, Nicklaus could not gain ground because of Player's consistency

and then, at the 13th, Nicklaus lost his last chance when he hooked his tee shot and went five down. Despite calling upon all his resources, the Golden Bear was powerless to prevent a Player victory.

By the time the 1967 Championship came around Player had been enduring a bad spell. His anxiety to win the British Open at Hoylake cost him dearly and his final round of 74 lost him the title. But he was still as determined as ever to do well at Wentworth. After all, it was beginning to look as though match-play golf was designed for Player.

With darkness approaching he won a titanic first-round battle with Gay Brewer at the 39th hole but was involved in a curious incident on the third, and last, extra hole when, after both men had played their drive, Brewer noticed the pin position had been altered in readiness for the next day's play. Brewer insisted on it being replaced to its original position before they played their second shots, and official Michael Bonallack had to cut

Left: *Gary Player (left) and Peter Thomson line up before the start of the 1965 Final. Player won 3 & 2.*

the original hole with a penknife borrowed from a member of the gallery! The re-siting of the hole was to no avail for Brewer as Player won the hole and the match. In the semi-final Peter Thomson gained revenge for his 1965 Final defeat with a 2 hole victory which ended at the 36th when Player went out of bounds.

The lack of confidence and tension shown by Player in 1967 was gone in 1968 when he came to Wentworth with renewed confidence after winning the British Open by two strokes from Jack Nicklaus at Carnoustie. Despite the dreadful weather conditions, the customary large gallery turned out at Wentworth to watch eight of the best of the world's golfers do battle for what was becoming one of the sport's most cherished titles outside the 'Majors.'

Once more the event continued its reputation for providing great matches and after a devastating first round 8 & 7 win over Peter Thomson, Player was engaged in a classic with Britain's Tony Jacklin.

Jacklin had trailed for most of the match, but kept coming back at the South African and as darkness fell over the Surrey course, Player had a simple four-foot putt for the match, but missed. Because of the lack of light, the extra holes were held over to the Saturday and Player won the first extra hole but was involved in an unpleasant incident with a female spectator who, displaying uncontrollable bias towards Jacklin, shouted 'Miss it! Miss it' as Player was about to putt. Player did not miss and went over to remonstrate with the woman immediately after making his putt. Jacklin then missed and lost the match. Many felt Player should have waited until after Jacklin had played before speaking to the woman.

Nevertheless, Player was in his third final in four years. His opponent was New Zealander Bob Charles, who had beaten a subdued Arnold Palmer in the semi-final. The two engaged in a close battle over 36 holes and Player went into the 36th with a one-hole lead. Charles, renowned for his accurate putting had a ten-footer to stay in the match. By his own high standards he would normally have made the putt but not this time, and Player went on to win his third title.

Charles gained compensation by beating Gene Littler in the 1969 Final as Player lost 4 & 3 to the delicate skills of Littler in the semi-final, but not until he had equalled the biggest winning margin in the championship in the first round after beating Frenchman Jean Garaialde 10 & 8.

Jack Nicklaus won his first (and only) title in 1970, but Player was not to be a threat as he lost to Tony Jacklin in the first round as one of the strongest ever fields assembled for the Championship. Player nearly missed the event because his father had been taken to hospital in South Africa. When Player was advised his condition was not as serious as first thought he decided to compete at Wentworth but there was more than a hint of suspicion that he had more than golf on his mind during his match with Jacklin.

Jacklin came off *his* sick bed to play in 1971 and he had the daunting prospect of a third meeting in four years with Player when the first round pairings put them together. It was Player's turn to win as he set up a victory by winning four of the first five holes after lunch. After beating Bob Charles 2 & 1 in the semi-final, Player booked himself a second final against Jack Nicklaus. The first 18 looked as though another of Wentworth's classics was on the cards as the players halved the first 11 holes. After lunch, however, Nicklaus lost his touch and Player won on the 32nd green, just as he had done when the two met in the 1966 Final.

Above: *Hale Irwin (left) and Gary Player both line up the same problem, but from different angles, during the 1974 Final.*

Left: *No play at Wentworth in 1968 for Player and Jacklin. When they did commence battle it was a 'classic' encounter.*

Player's match-play skills were second to none and his complete dedication to fitness helped him in a tournament that required 36-holes-a-day for three days. But the first round draw in 1972 paired him with Peter Oosterhuis who had proved himself a useful match-play golfer in the previous year's Ryder Cup with impressive wins over Gene Littler and Arnold Palmer in the singles. Oosterhuis took Player by storm as he went four up after five holes but, by the 13th of the afternoon session he had lost his lead. Few would have complained if he had gone on to lose the match but he showed fine character and came back at the great man. The Briton hit Player with a killer blow at the 34th hole when he sank a 16-foot putt. They halved the last two and Oosterhuis claimed a great victory and joined fellow Briton Tony Jacklin in the semi-final. Player was to get his revenge at Lytham two years later when he edged Oosty out of the British Open by two strokes.

The 1973 Championship was the 10th anniversary and Player had not only established himself as the best match-play golfer in the world but had also become the only one to compete in all ten championships. The pairing of Jacklin and Player once more dominated the first round draw and, as Jacklin was coming back to peak form, a great match was expected, but he could provide no opposition for the South African on the day as Player won 3 & 2. Another 3 & 2 win over Johnny Miller in the semi-final put Player in his fifth final where he met Australian Graham Marsh.

The 1973 Final was the 70th match since the championships were inaugurated, and it turned out to be one of the event's classics. Thousands of followers were absorbed in a thrilling contest in which it was unfortunate there had to be a loser. Neither player allowed the other to take command and there was never more than one in it during the morning round. They were all square at lunch but then Marsh won two of the first three after the break. Player was level after seven holes and *he* then went two up. Marsh then won the 15th and 16th to draw level again before Player won the 17th. Marsh showed little respect for the man who had made the Championship his 'own' by levelling the match at the 18th when all seemed lost. Four extra holes were needed before Player won the play-off at the 40th in the longest match in the history of the event, and Player took his earnings in the ten years of the championship to more than £40,000.

Player was still at his best when he returned in 1974. He easily beat Ben Crenshaw 4 & 3 in the first round, and then disposed of Jerry Heard in the semi-final, but then poor putting by Player and a better all-round performance by Hale Irwin in the final gave the American the first of his two successive titles. It was Player's first defeat in six final appearances and it turned out to be his last final.

Gary Player may have lost his crown after being dethroned as the match-play king, but he continued to show the golfing world he was not finished and was still capable of winning big titles, and in 1978 he showed many younger players he was not past it when he won the Masters at the age of 42. He is still a feared competitor.

Below: *Gene Littler inflicted one of Player's biggest World Match-Play defeats in the 1969 semi-final by 4 & 3.*

WORLD MATCH-PLAY CHAMPIONSHIP 1965-74
GARY PLAYER'S RESULTS

1965		
Round 1	beat	Neil Coles (GB) 5 & 4
Semi Final	beat	Tony Lema (USA) at 37th
Final	beat	Peter Thomson (Aus) 3 & 2
1966		
Round 1	beat	Neil Coles (GB) 1 hole
Semi Final	beat	Arnold Palmer (USA) 2 & 1
Final	beat	Jack Nicklaus (USA) 6 & 4
1967		
Round 1	beat	Gay Brewer (USA) at 39th
Semi Final	lost to	Peter Thomson (Aus) 2 holes
1968		
Round 1	beat	Peter Thomson (Aus) 8 & 7
Semi Final	beat	Tony Jacklin (GB) at 37th
Final	beat	Bob Charles (NZ) 1 hole
1969		
Round 1	beat	Jean Garaialde (France) 10 & 8
Semi Final	lost to	Gene Littler (USA) 4 & 3
1970		
Round 1	lost to	Tony Jacklin (GB) 2 holes
1971		
Round 1	beat	Tony Jacklin (GB) 4 & 3
Semi Final	beat	Bob Charles (NZ) 2 & 1
Final	beat	Jack Nicklaus (USA) 5 & 4
1972		
Round 1	lost to	Peter Oosterhuis (GB) 1 hole
1973		
Round 1	beat	Tony Jacklin (GB) 3 & 2
Semi Final	beat	Johnny Miller (USA) 3 & 2
Final	beat	Graham Marsh (Aus) at 40th
1974		
Round 1	beat	Ben Crenshaw (USA) 4 & 3
Semi Final	beat	Jerry Heard (USA) 5 & 4
Final	lost to	Hale Irwin (USA) 3 & 1

PLAYER'S THIRD MASTERS

Player had won two Masters titles before 1978. He beat Palmer and Charles Coe by one shot in 1961 to become the first overseas winner of the title and then, in 1974, he beat Dave Stockton and Tom Weiskopf by two strokes to lift his second title. Now, in 1978, he was ready to show how and why his desire for physical fitness would carry him through to his ninth 'Major'.

Still weighing the same 150 pounds as he did when he first won the Masters in 1961, Player was one of ten overseas professionals in the field, all of whom had to combat the strong home contingent that contained potential champions like Nicklaus, of course, Tom Watson and Lee Trevino, still looking for his first Masters title.

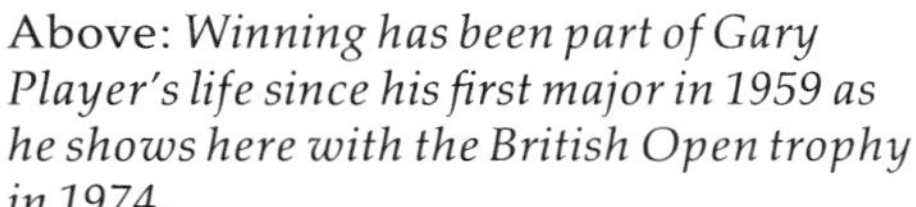

Above: *Winning has been part of Gary Player's life since his first major in 1959 as he shows here with the British Open trophy in 1974.*

Left: *The familiar all-black outfit of South Africa's most successful golfer, Gary Player.*

The first-round leader, however, was not one of the big names but former Rookie of the Year, 38-year-old John Schlee from Texas, who shot a four-under par 68. Nicklaus had a 72 as did Player, who returned two halves of 36. But the biggest threat seemed to come from Trevino who cut down on the clowning as he made a serious challenge for the elusive title with a 70.

As Schlee dropped from the limelight on day two Trevino certainly stepped into it by taking the joint lead on 139 with Rod Funseth who shot a great 66. Player shot a second successive 72 but was well down the field and five off the lead. He was seven off the lead, on 213, at the end of the third round after a 69 but he was now looking at a new leader, Hubert Green, who shot a 65, just one off the Championship record. Green enjoyed a three-stroke lead over Funseth and Tom Watson, who had emerged as a strong contender after a second successive 68.

Trevino's great play over the first 36 holes was undone at the easy fifth, when he shot a triple bogey seven.

A tight finish was expected on the final day, but there must have been few who imagined the small South African would storm through the field to win.

Player shot a blistering 64 to equal the course record and as he picked up strokes on the leaders it was obvious the Masters was heading for one of its closest ever finishes. At one stage during the second nine holes, the leaderboard showed Player, Green, Watson and Funseth all square. Player was first to complete his round and could do no more. He was in on 277 and the eventual outcome was now out of his hands. As each of the other three came to the 18th tee in turn, they were one behind Player, and each had putts to level the match and force a sudden-death play-off.

Above, left: *Tom Weiskopf finished second to Player when he won the 1974 Masters title.*

Above right: *The third-round leader Hubert Green who dropped eight shots to Player in the final round.*

1978 MASTERS

Scores after three rounds:	Scores after four rounds:
206 Hubert Green	277 GARY PLAYER
209 Tom Watson	278 Rod Funseth
209 Rod Funseth	278 Hubert Green
210 Gene Littler	278 Tom Watson
(213 Gary Player)	

Funseth had a 24-footer, but missed by inches. Watson had an easier putt from 12 feet, and he also missed. Then Green, with the easiest chance of all, from 30 inches, surprisingly missed as Player stood and watched in amazement as he became Masters Champion for the third time after trailing by seven shots at the start of the day. His final round of 64 was one of the Masters' great rounds, and worthy of taking the title, and was the lowest final round by a champion.

Player was presented with the coveted Green Jacket by Watson, the defending champion, as he became the oldest recipient of one of golf's most famous prizes.

This was Player's 19th win on the US circuit, and 112th world wide. He did not go on to win another Major but those who saw him in action at Augusta in 1978 could never discount

Above: *Trouble for Player at the 15th at Augusta after his ball ended up in the pond.*

Left: *'It still fits' – Tom Watson putting the coveted Green Jacket on Gary Player after the South African won his third Masters title in 1978.*

him from winning any future tournament.

Player, and Palmer, are now delighting American fans with their regular play on the Seniors Tour and help rekindle numerous memories they have built up during their long and great careers. Jack Nicklaus, on the other hand, is still competing regularly on the US Tour. Furthermore he is still capable of showing many a younger golfer a thing or two as he proved in 1986 when he won the Masters for the sixth time to prove that the second Great Triumvirate is alive and well.

LIFE BEYOND NICKLAUS, PALMER AND PLAYER

Yes, there *was* life beyond Nicklaus, Palmer and Player in the sixties and early seventies and despite the monopoly held by the Big Three, other golfers managed to steal their own share of the limelight. Britain's Tony Jacklin was in the spotlight twice, after winning the British and US Opens within a year, and then a new pair of American challengers emerged in the shape of Johnny Miller and Tom Watson. Hale Irwin threatened to become the next in the long line of greats and a man who was never far away from the headlines was Lee Trevino. Another man who could have threatened the triumvirate was Tony Lema, but a tragic aircraft disaster deprived the golf world of one of its great characters in 1966.

Two years before the disaster Lema had won the British Open at the first attempt. Furthermore it was his first ever tournament in Britain, and he had had little more than a day to prepare for the championship over the famous St Andrews links.

Left to right, Watson, Trevino and Jacklin

Tony Lema

Johnny Miller

'CHAMPAGNE TONY' ARRIVES

An ex-Marine, Lema had been on the US Tour five years and came close to his first 'Major' in 1963 when he lost the Masters by one stroke to Nicklaus. That was the first warning he posted to the rest of the golf world that 'Champagne Tony' was on his way. He acquired his nickname at the 1962 Orange County Open in California when he promised pressmen he would treat them to champagne if he won. He did, and he kept his promise and they penned him as 'Champagne Tony' after that. The nickname was not only known within the golf world because the US Wine Industry declared Lema their best salesman of 1965.

A strong American contingent made the trip to St Andrews for the 1964 Open and were hoping to redress the balance after New Zealander Bob Charles had beaten Phil Rodgers in a play-off at Lytham in 1963. Nicklaus and Palmer, who finished first and second in the Whitewash Tournament in Pennsylvania on the Sunday before the Open, flew direct from Philadelphia to Scotland and gave warnings during practice that they were to be treated as serious contenders for the title.

Strong winds of up to 65 miles per hour confused the Americans on the opening day, particularly on the greens and the leader board was headed by Frenchman Jean Garaialde and Irishman Christy O'Connor who enjoyed a one-stroke lead over Briton Harry Weetman and Australian Bruce Devlin.

The American challenge was led by Lema who was two off the lead and who, apart from finding sand at the 16th, had played a flawless round in appalling conditions. The confidence based on three recent wins on the US Tour was self evident as he adapted himself to his first round of tournament golf in Britain.

As Jack Nicklaus and his putter fell out on the second day Lema was the sole American left to challenge the overnight leaders and he swept into the lead with a 68 which put him two ahead of Weetman. Lema was driving superbly, and drove the 359-yard ninth. He could easily have returned a 63 because he had five birdie putts, all from around ten feet, all of which he failed to sink. Nicklaus, despite his problems with his putter, was still the next best-placed American, but was nine behind Lema.

Below: *Tony Lema shot an opening round of 73, but two rounds of 68 helped him win the British Open title in 1964.*

1964 BRITISH OPEN (TONY LEMA)	
Final scores:	
279 TONY LEMA	73-68-68-70
284 Jack Nicklaus	76-74-66-68
285 Roberto de Vicenzo	76-72-70-67
287 Bernard Hunt	73-74-70-70

The final day's play provided some of the most exhilarating golf ever seen over the famous Old Course as Lema and Nicklaus gave a display of golf at its highest level over the last 36 holes.

In the morning Nicklaus had a 66 and a lesser man than Lema would have crumbled with the Golden Bear on the rampage but Lema showed no signs of nerves and played his own game for a 68. Nicklaus had gained two but the afternoon was a formality as, right from the first hole, Lema showed he was not going to let it slip. Nicklaus made up two further strokes but the seven-stroke margin at the start of the final round was just too big and Lema won his first 'Major.'

The graceful swing of 30-year-old Lema was a joy to watch and his determination, as Nicklaus tried to make up ground in the third round, was more reminiscent of Nicklaus himself. When the pressure was on Lema responded with five successive threes, three of them birdies. Tony Lema had brought his own brand of fun to golf and he enjoyed a flamboyant lifestyle, much the same as Walter Hagen had done 40 years earlier. The sport lost a great friend in 1966 when Lema lost his life in a plane crash at Munster, a suburb of Chicago, Illinois.

Having competed in a PGA tournament at Akron the previous day he was flying to the Chicago-Lansing airport when the plane developed trouble. The pilot, mother of five, Mrs Doris Mullen, attempted to bring the craft down in a lake on the golf course at the Lansing Sportsman's Club, but the wing caught the ground and the plane burst into flames immediately. Lema's wife Betty, and Dr George Bard, were also in the plane and all aboard the craft perished.

Lema was only 32 at the time and it was ironic that the man who had delighted so many, including his own 'Lema's Legion,' should lose his life on a golf course.

Left: *'Champagne Tony' holds aloft the British Open trophy which he had just won at the first attempt.*

Below: *The graceful swing of Tony Lema. Sadly the golf world was deprived of his skills following a plane crash in 1966.*

TONY JACKLIN'S GREAT YEAR

Little did he know it at the time but Tony Jacklin's memorable double of British and US Opens in 1969 and 1970 was the foundation stone on which was built the British and European invasion on the golfing world a decade later. Youngsters suddenly wanted to emulate Jacklin as golf fever swept Britain and Europe and, in part because of Jacklin's exploits, stars like Peter Oosterhuis, Nick Faldo, Severiano Ballesteros, Bernhard Langer and Sandy Lyle became world-beaters.

Jacklin, the son of a train driver in a Scunthorpe steelworks, had a meteoric rise to stardom in the six years between turning professional and winning the British Open at Royal Lytham in 1969. He made the game look easy, but had a tendency to make errors, particularly on the greens. But a trip to the States in 1968 resulted in him making everybody aware that Britain had its first great golfer for many years when he became the first Briton to win a US Tour event after taking the Jacksonville Open. But more important than winning his first US tournament he learned to play golf the American way. He slowed down his occasionally erratic swing, and improved his putting stroke.

The lessons he learned in the States

him on from hole to hole. Jacklin never faltered and played with great confidence knowing he was on his way to winning the title, not for himself, but for all his British fans who would share his triumph with him.

As he stood on the 18th tee he knew he could not let the public down at this late stage. Many a man would have played the last hole with caution. Not Jacklin; he was oozing with confidence and he unleashed a monster drive that sailed between the waiting bunkers on either side of the fairway. That over with, the rest was a formality as he maintained his two-stroke lead over Charles.

The adoration from the fans was something never before seen on a British course as Jacklin became the first home winner since Max Faulkner in 1951. The fans had every right to be delighted because they came to Lytham half-expecting yet another

Above: *Jacklin eyes up a putt during the 1969 Open at Lytham. He became the first Briton for 18 years to win the title.*

Right: *One of the great British sporting moments, Tony Jacklin's 1969 British Open win.*

Left: *Jacklin at work during the 1970 Masters tournament*

had made him a better golfer yet, surprisingly, he went to Lytham without a win to his name in the 1969 season. But he looked a winner all the way as he ended an 18-year drought of British success in their own championship.

Jacklin's first British Open was in 1963, also at Lytham, when he finished well down the field behind the first left-handed winner, New Zealander Bob Charles. Ironically, the 1969 championship was to develop into a two-man battle between Jacklin and Charles. The New Zealander held a two-stroke lead over Jacklin on the first day, thanks to a 66 to Jacklin's 68. Charles gained another stroke after the second round to give him a two-round total of 135 to Jacklin's 138 but Jacklin shot a 70 to Charles' 75 on the third day and he took a two-stroke lead he was never to lose. Going into the final round the leader board was notable for the absence of American names as Argentinian Roberto de Vicenzo, Australian Peter Thomson and Irishman Christy O'Connor all joined Charles as the pursuers of the lone Englishman.

The final round was a head-to-head involving Charles and Jacklin who played together and the 25-year-old Briton showed no signs of letting up as the wave of national emotion carried

American victory but, on a course that has not yet seen a win by an American professional, the US golfers were put in the shade by the British and Commonwealth contingent and, for the first time in ten years, no American golfer finished in the top five.

Jacklin's win changed the complexion of golf in Britain and Europe. People who had never dreamed of playing the sport before took it up in an effort to match Jacklin's success. Of course, only a few managed to reach anything like his standards, but those who did can, in retrospect, look back to that day in 1969 as the springboard for the present-day prominence of European golfers. Jacklin gave the sport its best possible boost for its future security.

The 1968 Jacksonville Open win had been a special landmark in Jacklin's career and the American fans had

Right: *A third round of 66 brought the 1967 champion Roberto de Vicenzo into the reckoning in 1969.*

Below: *Tony Jacklin (left) and Johnny Miller at Augusta in 1971. Jacklin could not add a Masters title to his US Open win.*

Above: *A great moment for the whole Jacklin family to share as Tony, Vivien and Bradley show off the US Open trophy.*

warmed to him. He had won them over and was now ready to launch the strongest possible attack on their home-grown players in their championship. Jacklin, and his fellow Britons, had had to sit and watch for long enough while American golfers won the British Open year after year – he was now about to redress the balance. Jacklin had come close to winning his second US Tour event in 1970 when he lost a play-off to Pete Brown in the San Diego Open.

The Hazeltine Course at Chaska, Minnesota, was the scene of the 70th US Open, and it was honored to be staging its first major championship. The course, the second longest ever used for a USGA tournament, came in for a lot of criticism, and several players even withdrew. Dave Hill, who was to finish runner-up, was severely reprimanded and fined for his comments about the severe course that contained a high number of blind shots.

Bad weather did not make conditions any easier but Jacklin stood in a class of his own as he led from the first day to the last, was the only player to break par for the tournament, and became only the second man in the history of the tournament, after Lee Trevino in 1968, to break par in every round. Jacklin's winning margin of seven was the biggest since Jim Barnes beat Walter Hagen and Fred McLeod by nine in 1921. To make Jacklin's record more impressive, the best of the world's golfers were in the field and even the 'Big Three' of Palmer, Player and Nicklaus could not master the course – on the opening day they shot first round scores of 79, 80 and 81 respectively. Nicklaus' 81 was his worst ever score in the Open while Jacklin's scores of 71-70-70-70 were the envy of every golfer that week at Hazeltine.

Jacklin played great golf all week and gave a display of inspired putting, an aspect of his game which had let him down in the past. His only slight lapses were at the seventh and eighth on the last day but he never looked in danger of losing his overnight four-stroke lead. He overcame his temporary anxiety at the ninth when he holed a 30-footer for a birdie after driving into the rough. After that it was plain sailing and he even holed an 18-foot putt for a birdie at the 18th to extend his already massive lead. He became the first Englishman since Ted Ray in 1920 to win the title, and the first Briton since Harry Vardon in 1900 to hold both British and US Open titles simultaneously.

The trappings of success were great for Jacklin and his earning power increased well beyond the £4250 he won at Lytham. He could never match his great 12 months ever again although he came close to regaining his British Open title in 1971, but Lee Trevino had other ideas at Royal Birkdale that day. Although he won few tournaments in Britain and Europe after his great year, Jacklin did win his second Jacksonville Open in 1972 when he beat John Jacobs in a play-off.

Jacklin remains as popular as ever with the British fans and he had the thrill of sharing another great moment with his nation in 1985 as he led the European side to victory over the United States in the Ryder Cup at the Belfry.

Left: *Captaining the winning European Ryder Cup team in 1985 comes high on Tony Jacklin's personal list of achievements.*

1969 BRITISH OPEN (TONY JACKLIN)

280 TONY JACKLIN	68-70-70-72
282 Bob Charles	66-69-75-72
283 Peter Thomson	71-70-70-72
283 Roberto de Vicenzo	72-73-66-72

1970 US OPEN (TONY JACKLIN)

281 TONY JACKLIN	71-70-70-70
288 Dave Hill	75-69-71-73
289 Bob Lunn	77-72-70-70
289 Bob Charles	76-71-75-67

BRITISH WINNERS OF POST-WAR BRITISH OPENS

1947 Fred Daly
1948 Henry Cotton
1951 Max Faulkner
1969 Tony Jacklin
1985 Sandy Lyle

SUPER-MEX'S MEMORABLE 20 DAYS

Lee Trevino rarely likes to do things by half measures and when he won the Open Championships of the United States, Canada and Great Britain in 1971 he did so within a period of just 20 days.

When Trevino arrived at the Merion Club, Pennsylvania, for the US Open, he had victories in the Tallahassee Open and Danny Thomas-Memphis Classic under his belt and was confident of adding a second Open to his honors, to go with the one he had won at Oak Hill in 1968 – but there again, when was the last time Trevino was *not* confident?

If he was going to attack a course that still thrives on memories of Bobby Jones and Ben Hogan, he would have to cut the clowning and concentrate on accuracy throughout the 72 holes because Merion, although one of the shortest Open courses, does not allow any margin for error with its narrow fairways. Any course that was as testing as Merion must favor Jack Nicklaus and he was installed as the pre-tournament favorite. He was strongly fancied despite not having a win on the Tour leading up to the Open, but he had won the title at Oakmont in 1962 and Baltusrol five years later. Trevino had won his first Open in 1968, when he beat Nicklaus by four, and the two were ready to commence battle once again at Merion.

Trevino opened with a poor 37 on the first nine, but got his game together with a 33 on the inward nine for an opening round total of 70, three behind Labron Harris from Stillwater, Okla-

Above: *Super-Mex's confrontation with Mr Lu will be remembered for many years.*

Left: *Trevino pictured at Royal Birkdale, scene of the third leg of his great treble in 1971.*

homa who was certainly not among the list of potential winners discussed before the start of the tournament.

The second day was very strange. Nicklaus and Arnold Palmer moaned about the severe pin placements and slow play respectively but, at the end of the day both were in contention, three behind the new leaders Bob Erickson and Jim Colbert, while Super-Mex was one behind Palmer and Nicklaus.

Just when were the big names going to take over at the top of the leader board? Well, it was certainly not on the third day as 21-year-old Wake Forest College junior Jim Simons became the first amateur since Marty Flackman in 1967 to lead the Open after 54 holes. He must have been black-and-blue with pinching himself to make sure he was not dreaming. Nicklaus shot a 65 for 207 and a move into second place, two behind Simons. Trevino, who played the third round with Simons, shot a 69 and was four off the lead, but he was saving his fireworks for the final day.

Understandably the pressure got to the young amateur and, just as it looked as though Nicklaus was going to win his third title, Trevino sprinted through the last nine holes, as he had been doing all week, and carded another 33. Trevino's 69 was two better than Nicklaus so both finished on 280 which meant an 18-hole play-off the next day.

In a lightning-interrupted play-off Trevino looked the happier of the two men throughout. Nicklaus lost the chance of victory with two erratic bunker shots and Trevino increased his one-stroke lead at the half-way

TREVINO'S 20 DAYS

US OPEN
17-20 June (Merion)
280 TREVINO
280 Jack Nicklaus
(Trevino won play-off 68-71)

CANADIAN OPEN
1-4 July (Richelieu Valley)
275 TREVINO
275 Art Wall Jnr
(Trevino won play-off at 1st extra hole)

BRITISH OPEN
7-10 July (Royal Birkdale)
278 TREVINO
279 Liang Huan Lu
280 Tony Jacklin

stage to a winning margin of three at the end of 18 holes. Trevino had cut the clowning down, apart from one incident when he emerged from thick undergrowth with a rubber snake on the end of his club, and it certainly paid dividends for the likable Texan who was about to embark on the second leg of what was to be an historic treble.

That second leg took Trevino north of the border, to Montreal's Richelieu Valley course, and in contrast to his more serious behavior at Merion, he reverted to the clowning, particularly with the French-speaking locals who enjoyed his banter.

Trevino opened with a 73, six shots behind four Americans, Lou Graham, Rod Funseth, Phil Rodgers and Rolf Deming. But a 68 on the second day reduced the deficit to four behind a new leader, 47-year-old Art Wall who shot a great 67. Naturally, Trevino attracted one of the biggest galleries,

Left: *Not content with winning the three trophies in 1971 Lee also won the British Open the following year at Muirfield.*

Below: *Chipping like this has made Lee Trevino one of the best golfer s around the green.*

and when he was paired with the local man, Adrian Bigras, on day three that gallery was swelled even more. Many were hoping, of course, to see a local victory and thus put an end to the dominance the Americans had held since Pat Fletcher had last provided a home win in 1954.

Trevino had a great third round and took control on the par-threes, with three birdie twos in his record-equalling round of 67. He had a birdie chance at the 18th for a 66 but played to the right of the green instead of the left. When asked why he played his second to the wrong side of the green Trevino jokingly said: 'I played to the right because I asked my caddie where the pin was – and he said the left. . .!'

Wall, the 1960 champion, clung on to his lead with a 69 and was a tournament leader after three rounds for the first time since the 1966 Hartford Open. It would certainly have been a great win for the Pennsylvanian and with

Above: *Trevino holds aloft the giant US PGA trophy in 1984. The only one of the big four titles that has eluded him is the Masters.*

Strangely the British bookmakers ignored Trevino's run of success, and installed Nicklaus as the favorite. Perhaps that made sense in view of Big Jack's past British Open form and great love for British courses. Nicklaus had won the British Open twice and was the defending champion, while Trevino was looking for his first win in the tournament.

Britain's own Tony Jacklin was hoping to bring back the glory to himself, and his country, by regaining the title he had won just a few miles up the Lancashire coast in 1969 and was, with Trevino, one of four joint leaders on 69 after the first day. Nicklaus finished the day on 71 after a devastating outward half of 32, but he had two sixes in his inward half. Trevino was playing like a man who knew nothing but victory and his putting was the best part of his game as he made single putts on nine greens.

Jacklin and Trevino still shared center stage after both returned 70s on the second day, but the American only just kept himself in it with a 40-foot putt for an eagle three at the 18th. Just one behind the two leaders on 140 was Taiwan's Lu Liang Huan, who turned out to be the surprise packet of the 1971 Open. His play and manners delighted the Birkdale crowd as much as

Left: *A birdie at the 12th during the US Open play-off against Nicklaus that virtually assured Super-Mex of the title.*

Below: *Jack Nicklaus was on his way to his third US Open title until Trevino came with a late burst.*

nine holes to play he was still two up. But Trevino surged with another great challenge when all seemed lost, and had three birdies to Wall's one and forced a play-off after a superb final round of 67.

The play-off was sudden death and started – and finished – at the 410-yard tenth. Trevino drove into the rough but recovered with a wedge to 18 feet and then destroyed Wall by holing out for a birdie and the championship, reminding Wall of the 1967 Canadian Championship when he lost to Billy Casper in a play-off. Trevino packed his bags almost immediately to set off for England and the British Open at Birkdale with the advance warning to the British fans that Super-Mex was on his way.

With Trevino in full flight after becoming only the second man after Tommy Armour to win the Canadian and US titles in one year, the British fans had to take full notice of his intentions to become the first man to win all three Opens in one year.

Above: *Twenty-one-year-old amateur Jim Simons led the 1971 US Open after 54 holes but the pressure got to him on the final day.*

Trevino's wit. And when Mr Lu and Trevino were paired together for the final round, after Trevino shot a third round 69 to take the outright lead by one from Lu and Jacklin, the vast crowd was delighted.

After shooting an outward 31 in which he single putted six greens, Trevino extended his lead over Lu, who was powerless to do anything. Jacklin slipped away but recovered in the second nine while Lu continued to play steady golf in the hope that Trevino would make a mistake. That mistake came at the 17th when he was three in front.

Trevino drove into a bunker, and failed to get out at the first attempt. When he did eventually get out he found deep rough on the opposite side of the fairway. After hitting the green he then three-putted for a seven while Lu made the par five. Lu was in with a chance but still needed to get a stroke back at the last hole, but it was to no avail as Trevino pulled himself together again. Trevino was a worthy winner of the 100th British Open, but Mr Lu was a worthy runner-up and as honorable in defeat, as Trevino was in victory.

Trevino joined the greats, Bobby Jones, Gene Sarazen and Ben Hogan, as winners of the British and US Opens in the same year. But he stood alone as the only man to add the Canadian Open to that list. Furthermore, he did it in the space of just 20 days to mark one of golf's great achievements, the like of which had not been seen since Bobby Jones' Grand Slam Year in 1930.

1975 – THE GREATEST OF ALL MASTERS

Although life did extend beyond Palmer, Player and Nicklaus in the 1970s, it was hard to ignore Nicklaus as he was still very much part of the golf scene, and was waiting to show his young pretenders that he was not prepared to surrender his crown easily. And when it came round to Masters time each spring, Nicklaus was as determined as ever to show who was the real 'King of Augusta.'

If Nicklaus epitomizes golf's greatness, then he feels the same way about the Masters and regards it as his favorite of all 'Majors' – hardly surprising therefore that he had won the title four times before he started his challenge in 1975.

Johnny Miller was being hailed as the 'New Nicklaus,' Hubert Green was also a new pretender waiting to steal some of Nicklaus' glory and old stager Tom Weiskopf was enjoying a newfound confidence after winning the Greater Greensboro Open. The stage was set and the course was as immaculate as ever and ready to taunt and tease the best players in the world.

Heavy rain had made the normally fast greens slower than usual and there were many sub-par rounds on the opening day including a 68 from Nicklaus, which was one off Bobby Nichols' lead. Weiskopf shot a 69 but Miller was way down on 75. Even Sam Snead, the 'Geriatric Wonder' as he was described, shot a 71. But Nicklaus gave a one-man show on the second day with a blistering 67 for a total of 135 and a five-stroke lead, a rare feat, even for Nicklaus, at the end of just two days' play. Billy Casper, Tom Watson and Arnold Palmer were all tied second on 140 while the men with whom Nicklaus was to engage in a great battle on the final day, Weiskopf and Miller, were on 141 and 146 respectively.

A five-stroke lead for Nicklaus might seem like giving him the key to Fort Knox; well, it would normally but for some inexplicable reason he ended the third day one behind Weiskopf after a 73 to Weiskopf's 66. Johnny Miller dragged himself into the spotlight with a Masters record of six consecutive birdies for a 65 and a three-round total of 211, four behind the new leader. So,

Left: *Jack Nicklaus just managed to hold on to win a record fifth Masters in 1975.*

Above: *Closing rounds of 65-66 nearly brought Johnny Miller his first Masters – a title he has still not won.*

Left: *The third character from 'The Greatest Masters of All' – Tom Weiskopf. Like Miller he never won the title, but was runner-up four times.*

Three studies of Jack Nicklaus: (above left) joy at making a birdie at the 16th, (left) putting on the famous Green Jacket for the fifth time and (above right) apprehensively watching Tom Watson.

THE GREATEST MASTERS OF ALL – 1975

	Round One	Round Two	Round Three	Final Score
Nicklaus	68	135	208	276
Miller	75	146	211	277
Weiskopf	69	141	207	277

with one round to go, and the scores reading: Weiskopf 207, Nicklaus 208, Miller 211, the large Augusta crowd wondered what the final day had in store. The answer . . . one of the most exciting climaxes to the Masters in its 41-year history.

Nicklaus orchestrated proceedings as he and Weiskopf took it in turn to take the lead while Miller, despite birdies at 15 and 17 to get within one stroke, could never overtake the other two. Nicklaus sunk a monster 40-footer that broke two ways before going down at the 16th to strike a deadly body-blow to his opponents. He made par at the 18th after missing a birdie chance to finish with a 68 for a final total of 276. Weiskopf and Miller both teed off at the 18th one behind Nicklaus – either, or both, needed a birdie three to stay alive.

Miller hit a nine-iron second shot which left him with a 20-footer for his birdie while Weiskopf put his second to within eight feet. Miller, first of all, missed his difficult putt. Then to Weiskopf's absolute horror, his putt, although dead on line, stopped on the lip of the cup and he finished runner-up for the fourth time, and third time in four years. For Nicklaus it was the fifth time he had had the privilege of putting the famous Green Jacket on his back. He certainly showed he was not to be written off either before, or during a competition, particularly when the competition in question is the Masters.

MILLER--A THREAT TO NICKLAUS?

The arrival of Johnny Miller in the early seventies took the golf world by storm and he was widely tipped as the natural successor to Nicklaus. Many predicted he would be winning tournaments for a long time to come and between 1971 and 1976 he won 20 tournaments world wide and in 1973 he won his first 'Major' when he beat John Schlee by one to win the US Open after a remarkable final round of 63. It was that sort of golf that won him eight Tour events the following year and then in 1975 he started the year with consecutive wins in the Phoenix Open and Tucson Open when he carded a 61 each time in winning with scores in excess of 20-under par.

For sheer excitement though, Miller could not have had a more testing time than his victory in the 1976 British Open at Royal Birkdale when he had to

Above: *Miller receives the British Open championship trophy after his win at Royal Birkdale in 1976.*

Opposite page: *Johnny Miller was hailed as the 'new Jack Nicklaus' for a time.*

outplay a young, little-known, Spaniard on the final round to turn a two-stroke deficit into a six-stroke winning margin. That Spaniard was Severiano Ballesteros.

As Britain was going through its hottest summer of the century the 7000-yard Birkdale course was playing easier than usual and British Open records were clearly in peril of being broken. The fine weather brought fans in their thousands to the west coast course and a first-day record 17,000 saw Miller, Tom Weiskopf, and Jack Nicklaus, all pre-tournament favorites, have trouble with the fast greens. Miller, in particular, was spoiling a great round with his putting and required 34 putts in his round of 72. Nicklaus, playing on his least favorite British Open course, was two behind.

The long dry summer brought the inevitable hazard of fire and a couple of minor outbreaks during the practice rounds were followed by a more severe one among the gorse and shrub alongside the first fairway which caused a half-hour delay to the proceedings. But, once play got under way and the first day's leaders were posted, the names of Christy O'Connor junior, Suzuki of Japan – who received a lot of pre-tournament publicity – and Severiano Ballesteros – who warranted very little publicity before the start of the tournament – appeared at the top of the board on 69.

While the field had a distinctive international flavor to it there was only one Spaniard in the tournament and the 19-year-old Ballesteros gave a brilliant display of long-iron play in his opening round. He then amazed everybody with a second round, also of 69, as he went into a two-stroke lead over Miller while Nicklaus was six behind the Spaniard. Ballesteros showed great maturity, particularly after he temporarily lost his share of the lead but then came back strongly even with men like Miller, Nicklaus, reigning Masters champion Ray Floyd, and Hubert Green all waiting for him to make a mistake.

While Ballesteros relied on his long irons so did Miller – he took his trusty one-iron out of his bag ten times, and it never once let him down. Nor did his new driver, which he had changed overnight, as he played his way to a course record 68 which only stood for a few minutes before fellow Americans Higgins, and then Ray Floyd, shot brilliant 67s.

Miller and Ballesteros both shot 73s in the third round and the youngster held on to his two-stroke lead, much to the amazement of many pundits who predicted he would 'blow up.' Ballesteros had little intention of cracking as he brought a new excitement to the game which he played with great enjoyment and youthful verve. He took chances, but somehow always seemed to get away with it when disaster loomed. That sort of luck, allied to his great natural talent, is an ideal ingredient for British Open success.

On a mixed day, the two leaders had the best of the weather, but could not capitalize and open up a gap at the top of the leader board. Ballesteros had a disastrous three-putt at the first green and covered the first nine in 38 while Miller went out in 34 to take the lead.

Above: *Severiano Ballesteros (in the rough) and Johnny Miller in battle during the 1976 British Open at Royal Birkdale.*

Right: *The victory leap says it all and the large Birkdale gallery shares Miller's delight.*

1976 BRITISH OPEN

Scores at the end of Round Three
211 Severiano Ballesteros
213 JOHNNY MILLER
215 Tommy Horton
216 Jack Nicklaus
216 Ray Floyd
Final Scores
279 JOHNNY MILLER
285 Jack Nicklaus
285 Severiano Ballesteros
286 Ray Floyd

But then Ballesteros returned in 35 to Miller's 39 and stamped his authority at the 17th with an eagle. But, while all eyes were on the two leaders, that wily old fox, Nicklaus, played a steady round in bad conditions to gain a stroke on Miller and Ballesteros with a 72 which gave him a three-round total of 216.

The widely predicted crash of Ballesteros came on the final day when Miller took the lead at the sixth. The Spaniard dropped three strokes with a seven at the 11th and Miller took complete control with a two at the 12th. From there on it was one-way traffic and Ballesteros did well to hang on for a tie for second place with Nicklaus who threw away his chance with a six that followed two birdies.

Miller added the British Open to his US title and recalled that, like Ballesteros, he nearly won his first 'Major,' the 1971 Masters, when still a 'novice.' That loss, he felt, had done him no harm, and he suggested that Ballesteros would benefit from his defeat.

The 1976 British Open was something of a swansong for Johnny Miller as he started to slide down the US money list, but that decline coincided with his decision to spend more time with his wife Linda and their six children as he put his family before the sport.

WATSON--THE REAL THREAT TO NICKLAUS

Above: *Jack Nicklaus (right) with his 'heir apparent' at Turnberry in 1977.*

Miller was just one of the men hailed as a possible successor to Jack Nicklaus, but one player who became more than a 'possible' was Tom Watson, who soon developed into a 'probable.'

A former Stanford University student, Watson graduated in 1971 with a degree in psychology but decided to turn to his first love, golf, and joined the professional ranks that same year. It was a long hard slog to begin with but the breakthrough came in 1974 when he won the Western Open. Since then he has won more than 30 Tour events including the US Open in 1982 and the Masters in 1977 and 1981 but in the eight years between 1975 and 1983 he had no equal in the British Open winning the title five times, just one short of Harry Vardon's all-time record.

Watson's first triumph was on Scotland's beautiful Carnoustie links in 1975 when he beat the unfortunate Australian Jack Newton by one stroke in an 18-hole play-off. At Muirfield five years later he beat Lee Trevino by four shots thanks to the assistance of a third round 64, and at Troon in 1982 he beat Britain's Peter Oosterhuis and South Africa's Nick Price by one stroke after he had built a five-stroke lead over the Briton on the first round. He laid his bogey of not being able to win in England in 1983 when he beat Hale Irwin and Andy Bean by one over the tough Royal Birkdale links but his greatest triumph was at Turnberry in 1977 in the first championship which had been played over the famous west of Scotland links.

With the famous Ailsa Craig and the Mull of Kintyre making the ideal backdrop for such an occasion, Tom Watson and Jack Nicklaus engaged in one of the best head-to-head challenges over four rounds in the history of the Open as they shattered records along the way. The course was playing easy, but the fluctuating winds which can make the famous course hazardous and can change its entire character within minutes were a threat. But Watson and Nicklaus dominated the course and returned four round totals of 268 and 269. Watson's winning total wiped eight strokes off the championship record, and the pundits who belittle the success of Watson and Nicklaus because of the ease of the course should not lose sight of the fact that third placed Hubert Green was 11 shots behind Watson.

Low scoring on the first day set the pattern for the entire competition and John Schroeder, son of former Wimbledon tennis champion Ted Schroeder, set the championship alight with a 66 while Watson and Nicklaus both started with 68s. Mark Hayes established a new Open record 63 on the second day which saw Nicklaus and Watson again level, but this time on 70 for a total of 138, the same as Hubert Green and Lee Trevino, but that formidable quartet was one behind the new leader Roger Maltbie.

It was evident after the first two day's low scoring that more records would be added to Hayes' new championship best, and Watson and Nicklaus were both to create a new championship low for three rounds with a pair of 65s on the third day. They

Left: *The faces do not give any clues as to where the ball went, but judging by the swing – straight down the middle.*

Below: *Watson keeping an eye on Nicklaus' shot during the record-breaking 1977 British Open at Turnberry.*

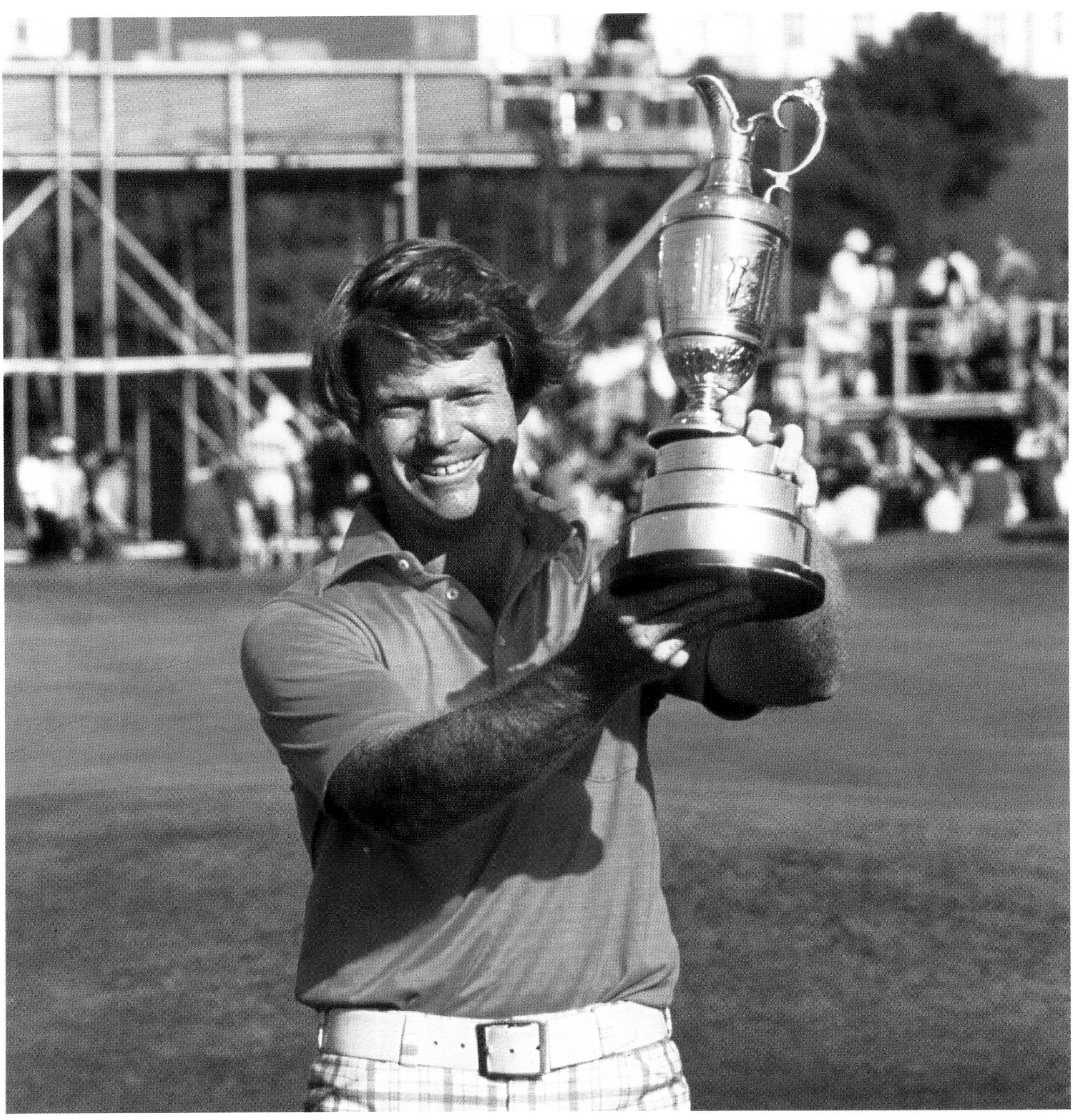

1977 BRITISH OPEN AT TURNBERRY

Final scores:

268 TOM WATSON	68-70-65-65
269 Jack Nicklaus	68-70-65-66
279 Hubert Green	72-66-74-67

Previous low British Open totals:
276 Arnold Palmer (Troon, 1962)
276 Tom Weiskopf (Troon, 1973)
277 Bob Charles (Lytham, 1963)
277 Phil Rodgers (Lytham, 1963)

had built up a three-stroke lead over Ben Crenshaw in a day interrupted by lightning and rain and set up a great finish to the first championship at Turnberry.

The final day saw the initiative change hands several times, first to Nicklaus, who was three shots to the good after four holes but then Watson levelled it at the eighth before dropping a shot at the ninth. Nicklaus increased his lead to two at the 12th but three holes later they were level with three to play. They both made fours at the 16th but then Watson had a birdie four at the 17th to Nicklaus' par and after both making threes at the 18th Watson was Champion for the second time in a truly remarkable finish.

Although the course played easy and records were shattered, they were only broken because two men could manage to put together four consistent rounds – only great players can do that. Nicklaus, in finishing second for the sixth time, did not need to prove how great he was – his record did that. But Watson proved that in taking on, and beating, the great man he was ready to succeed Nicklaus as 'King.'

Turnberry's Records in 1977:

- Lowest winning score – 268 Watson
- Lowest score by runner-up – 269 Nicklaus
- Lowest individual round – 63 Mark Hayes
- Lowest second round – 63 Mark Hayes
- Lowest final round – 65 Watson (equalled record)
- Lowest final round by a champion – 65 Watson
- Most rounds under 70 – There were 40 sub-70 rounds
- Lowest score over last 36 holes – 130 (65 & 65) Watson
- Lowest score over first 54 holes – 203 (68, 70 & 65) Nicklaus & Watson
- Lowest score over the final 54 holes – 200 (70, 65 & 65) Watson

Left: *After a titanic four-day battle, Tom Watson emerged as the winner of Turnberry's first Open thanks to a 65 in the final round to Jack Nicklaus' 66 – the only stroke that separated them all week.*

Right: *Watson during the 1982 British Open at Troon.*

Below: *Craig Stadler and caddie Alfie Fyles rush over to congratulate Watson after his fifth British Open win in 1983.*

HALE IRWIN'S CHANCE

When Hale Irwin 'arrived' in 1974 he came as the man who combined Jack Nicklaus' will to win with the fact that he was one of the game's great shotmakers. It was the emergence of another champion.

Irwin has enjoyed a long and successful career since winning the NCAA championship in 1967. He turned professional the following year and rose from 117th in the money list in 1968 to 13th in 1971 when he had his first Tour win, the Heritage Classic. The Classic also provided him with his second Tour win two years later but his third win, in 1974, was the first highlight of his career as he won the US Open by two shots from Forest Fezler.

The 6961-yard, par 70 West Course at Winged Foot, complete with its super-fast greens, was the scene of Irwin's first great moment. It had no weaknesses to offer and was ready to 'eat up' the unsuspecting golfer.

South African Gary Player was the only man to make par on the opening day, one stroke ahead of Arnold Palmer's ex-caddie Mike Reasor, and former presidential guard, Lou Graham. Irwin shot a 36 and 37 for an opening 73 while defending champion Johnny Miller struggled to make 76. Gary Player lost six strokes on the first six holes of the second round and high scoring was again commonplace with four men sharing the lead on 143, three over par. Seasoned campaigners Player, Arnie Palmer and Ray Floyd were joined in the lead by Irwin. It was the first time since 1955 that a score as poor as three-over had led the Open . . . that's how tough Winged Foot was. Hubert Green, however, would disagree because he shot a 67 . . . mind you, he shot 81 the previous day!

Player went to ten-over 220 after a disastrous third round 77, Floyd went to 221 after a 78, and Palmer shot a 73 for 216. Irwin was the best of the overnight leaders after a 71, which included four three-putts, but he was still four over and one behind the new leader Tom Watson, who was looking for his first professional win.

Irwin was obviously feeling the pressure, but so was Watson. It was fortunate for the pair of them that Palmer could not stamp his authority on proceedings as victory was there for the taking. But in the end the outcome was decided as a result of Irwin and Watson trading mistakes.

Irwin drew level with Watson at the fifth and then broke away after a 40-foot putt went in. He never lost the lead after that and Watson started a bad run which included nine bogeys in his final 18-hole total of 79. Forest Fezler was capitalizing on the errors of the two leaders and got to within one of Irwin by the time he reached the 12th but he could not sustain the challenge as Irwin went on to win with a final

Below: *Hale Irwin served notice in the early-1970s that he could emerge as one of the biggest names in golf.*

Above: *Irwin during the 1979 British Open at Lytham.*

Left: *Former Presidential Guard Lou Graham was just one off the lead after the opening round of the 1974 US Open, but rounds of 74-75 then cost him dearly.*

round of 73 containing six bogeys and three birdies. His winning total of 287 was seven over par but the real winner was the course. Yet Irwin's win cannot be devalued by the high scoring because he had to pull away from Player, Palmer and Floyd before gaining victory, and that is never easy to do.

Five years later Irwin won his second title and once again he failed to break par for the championship but, by the time he won that second title at Inverness, Hale Irwin, the former defensive back in the University of Colorado football team, had built himself a reputation for being a great stylist and

consistent player. From early 1975 to the end of the 1978 US Tour he went 86 tournaments without missing the 36-hole cut and he regularly figured in the top ten money on the list. He was fast becoming a much feared man but, surprisingly, when he arrived at Inverness, Toledo, for the 1979 Open, he had not won on the US Tour since the 1977 San Antonio Open and a win was long overdue. Despite his lack of wins, he was still a consistent earner and set a record in 1978 for most prizemoney, $191,666, by a player without a tournament win.

It was the fourth Open to be held at Inverness. The first was in 1920 when Britain's Ted Ray won and the legendary Harry Vardon, in a severe gale, finished the last seven holes in level fives after leading by five strokes.

The par-71 course measured a demanding 6982 yards but one man who thought he had found a way of 'beating' the course was Lon Hinkle who shared the first-round lead on 70 thanks to an unusual birdie four at the par-five dog-leg eighth. Much to the embarrassment of the organizers he found it easier to drive down the adjacent 17th fairway which made the hole effectively a par four. Several other players followed Hinkle's ploy but were thwarted the next day when they arrived to find a tree planted in front of the teeing ground making the drive to the 17th fairway difficult, if not impossible.

With or without the aid of a short cut at the eighth most players found the course tough and only five of the 153 starters broke par. It was the first time since 1974, when Irwin first won the title, that no man had a score in the 60s and the big names were struggling. Watson, the top money-winner, and the sport's hottest property shot a 75, Trevino was home in 77, as was defending champion Andy North. Also on 77 was Masters champion Fuzzy Zoeller and reigning PGA title holder John Mahaffey. So Irwin's 74 looked respectable.

Watson, who started the Open as the strongest favorite for years, missed the 36-hole cut with a second round six-over par 77. Irwin, and Larry Nelson, shot the best rounds of the day – 68, and Nelson shared a three-shot lead over Irwin with Tom Purtzer. But Irwin was ready to pounce and a great third-round 67 gave him a three-stroke lead over Tom Weiskopf, who also shot a 67. Irwin got increasingly frustrated as the day went on because he could not shake off Weiskopf's challenge despite five birdies and an eagle, but Weiskopf gave a great display of putting that kept up his attack. Both men agreed that on the final day both would have to attack, and Irwin knew he could not sit back on his lead and hope par, or thereabouts, would win the day ... but to quote the old adage: 'Golf really is a funny game ...'

Left: *After an 18-year professional career Hale Irwin has won $2,811,034 on the US Tour (to the end of 1986).*

Above: *Despite gaining three shots on Irwin in the final round of the 1979 US Open, Jerry Pate could not make up the five-shot deficit.*

HALE IRWIN'S TWO US OPENS

1974 Open – Final scores:	
287 HALE IRWIN	73-70-71-73
289 Forest Fezler	75-70-74-70
290 Lou Graham	71-75-74-70
290 Bert Yancey	76-69-73-72.

1979 Open – Final scores:	
284 HALE IRWIN	74-68-67-75
286 Jerry Pate	71-74-69-72
286 Gary Player	73-73-72-68

The final round was reminiscent of his final round at Winged Foot in 1974 when, once again, it was not stunning play that won Irwin the title, but bad play by both him and, fortunately, his rivals. He finished with a 75 after dropping three shots on the last two holes and his round was the worst final round by a champion since 1949. Weiskopf had an even more disastrous round with a 76 and, had Gary Player's overnight deficit of nine strokes on Irwin not been so great, he could have won after a great closing round of 68. Instead Player tied for second with Jerry Pate. Irwin was never really threatened and, had he been, he might well have turned the pressure back on his rivals. But, in the words of Gary Player, 'The best man won.'

Irwin ended his 20-month drought and joined a select band of 13 other golfers to win two US Opens. Today, as Irwin approaches his 20th year on the US Tour, he can still be considered a threat in any tournament, and he certainly gave the impression in the mid-to-late seventies that he was going to be around a long time as he added further proof that life did exist beyond Palmer, Player and Nicklaus.

...AND SO TO THE PRESENT ERA

As we've journeyed through seventy glorious years of golf, comparisons are inevitable. Was Nicklaus as good as Jones? How did Player compare as a match-play golfer to Hagen? And who captured the public's imagination more, Hogan or Palmer?

Such comparisons are unfair but, as in all sports, are constantly made. The present era is no exception as the rising stars are compared with favorites of the past. But there is no doubting that golf has continued to enjoy a healthy life throughout the eighties with the appearance of such great players as the European pair of Severiano Ballesteros and Bernhard Langer who have shown that European golfers are now capable of taking on and beating the best of the Americans. That was never more evident than that September day at the Belfry, Sutton Coldfield, in 1985 when America lost its 28-year grip on the Ryder Cup. But the European invasion really started at Augusta five years earlier when the young Spaniard Ballesteros made the European breakthrough in the Masters.

Bernhard Langer

Severiano Ballesteros

Greg Norman

Bob Tway

BALLESTEROS BREAKS THROUGH

Above: *The familiar sight of Severiano Ballesteros successfully powering himself out of trouble.*

Right: *Marvellous touch and judgment form an equally important part of Seve's repertoire.*

Ballesteros, who had his 23rd birthday on the first day at Augusta in 1980 had been setting Europe alight since he won his first professional tournament, the 1976 Dutch Open. Since then he had headed the European money list in three successive years, culminating in a great three-stroke victory over Jack Nicklaus and Ben Crenshaw in the 1979 British Open at Royal Lytham. He had, a year earlier, given the American public a glimpse of his rare talent when he won the Greater Greensboro Open. Now, in 1980, they were about to discover the true talent of the youngster from Pedrena in northern Spain.

Overnight rain and a brisk wind made playing conditions difficult but Ballesteros, David Graham and Jeff Mitchell all managed to return opening rounds of 66 and, considering only 18 men broke par, to be six under was quite an achievement in such conditions. Ballesteros was driving better than ever and, in comparison to his erratic driving during his British Open victory at Lytham a year earlier when he was forced to play some outstanding recovery shots, he only missed one of Augusta's 18 fairways.

The Spaniard added a 69 on the second day but he had to call upon his full repertoire of recovery shots after returning to his wayward habits off the tee. But if anybody can invent a shot for an occasion then Ballesteros is the man, and the American fans were comparing him to the young Arnold Palmer who also had a disregard for obstacles and hazards as he thrashed his way around the course. Ballesteros had six birdies in his round and four of them came from tee shots that failed to find the fairway – that is recovery at its best.

He extended his four-shot lead to

Above: *Ben Crenshaw shared second place with Jack Nicklaus in the 1979 British Open as the Americans gave way to the young Spaniard.*

Above, top: *Seve celebrates his British Open success – Royal Lytham in 1979.*

Left: *Ballesteros (putting) on his way to his first US Tour win, the 1978 Greater Greensboro Open. Lanny Wadkins looks on.*

seven on the third day with another great round; this time it was flawless as he got it together again with his driver and hit 17 of the 18 fairways for a 68 and 13 under par. Few men had opened with three rounds under 70 in the Masters but Seve would have needed little reminding that Ed Sneed did so the previous year and eventually lost a three-way play-off after a disastrous 76 in the final round. On that occasion

Above: *Ballesteros receives his second Masters Green Jacket in 1983 from 'The Walrus,' Craig Stadler.*

Right: *Fuzzy Zoeller is the 'tailor' as Ballesteros gets his first Green Jacket in 1980.*

Sneed had Tom Watson, Tom Kite and Jack Nicklaus in pursuit. Ballesteros was a little more fortunate in that no big names were close to him, which made his task in the last 18 holes that much easier.

As Arnold Palmer can testify, after his 1960 and 1966 US Open performances, a seven-shot lead can soon evaporate but, when Ballesteros increased his lead to ten in the final round victory looked certain for the youngster. But, when that lead shrunk after three-putting the tenth for a bogey, finding Rae's Creek at the 12th for a double bogey, and finding another part of the creek at the 13th for another bogey, his lead was cut to just two shots over Gibby Gilbert who had been picking up birdies.

Gilbert could not expect the Spani-

Above: *Ballesteros during the 1983 Masters. The look on his face typifies his determination.*

ard to continue his bad streak and he did not. He gained two more shots on Gilbert and his final round of par-72 gave him victory by four strokes and, overall, he gave one of the best and most exhilarating performances seen in the Masters. He became the first European to win the title, and the only non-American other than Gary Player to wear the famous Green Jacket.

Ballesteros went on to win the title again in 1983 but the 1980 win at Augusta paved the way for the start of a European assault on the Americans in their own back yard and West Germany's Bernhard Langer was next to prove how strong European golf was in the 1980s.

1980 US MASTERS

Final scores:

275 SEVERIANO BALLESTEROS	66-69-68-72
279 Gibby Gilbert	70-74-68-67
279 Jack Newton	68-74-69-68
280 Hubert Green	68-74-71-67

BALLESTEROS' MAJOR CHAMPIONSHIP VICTORIES

1979 British Open
1980 US Masters
1983 US Masters
1984 British Open

LANGER'S TURN

Langer first realized he could play golf in the States when he shared the lead during the back nine on the last day of the World Series of Golf at the Firestone Country Club in 1981. Although he finished in a tie for sixth place that day, the feeling was good, and he knew he had proved himself capable of playing with the best in the world and, until you can do that against them, and on American soil, there must always be a lingering doubt.

He had proved himself a worthy challenger to Ballesteros as the leading European golfer since the day he won the prestigious Dunlop Masters in 1980 – in addition he was top money winner in Europe in 1981 and 1984. But he still had to emulate Ballesteros, and win in the States.

Langer's first serious assault on the US Tour was in 1985, prior to which his best performance had been third in the 1984 Bay Hill Classic, just one shot behind Gary Koch and George Burns. But now, despite not having a win to his credit in 1985, he was about to embark on his finest hour. Watson and Ballesteros were the two favorites for the 49th Masters but Jack Nicklaus had

Left: *The best player to emerge from West Germany, Bernhard Langer.*

Right: *Langer displays the correct way to play a delicate chip over a bunker.*

Below, right: *Curtis Strange opened the 1985 Masters with an 80, but shot a superb 65 in the second round. He finished joint third on 284.*

Below: *The large gallery anxiously awaits the outcome of Bernhard Langer's tee shot.*

Left: *American Payne Stewart reviving clothing styles of yesteryear – apart from the bright colors.*

gone into a week-long intensive practice session, hoping to make up for his unhappy 1984 tournament when he finished tied in 18th place.

Tom Watson was the first of the favorites to show on the opening day when he shot a 69, one behind the leader, the fedora-wearing Gary Hallberg, who brought back fond memories of Mr Lu at Royal Birkdale in 1971. Langer shot a level par 72, so did Ballesteros who missed more fairways and greens than he hit . . . once more his brilliance with the recovery shot saved him.

Langer shot a two-over 74 on the

Left: *Another birdie for Langer on his way to the 1985 Masters title.*

Above: . . . *and yet another.*

second day for a two-round total of 146 and was six behind the three-way leaders Craig Stadler, Payne Stewart and Watson. Ballesteros was three ahead of Langer after a 71 but the most amazing round of the day belonged to Curtis Strange who hammered the course with a 65 – the previous day the course hammered him as he shot 80.

Strange, the leading money winner, had a 68 in the third round and was on the verge of pulling off an amazing win particularly after that first round, but he still had to overhaul Ray Floyd who was the new leader, one ahead of Strange. Langer shot his best round of the tournament, 68, to move two behind the leader on 214, the same as Ballesteros. While the two outstanding Europeans had their eye on the two leading Americans, Lee Trevino and Tom Watson were keeping a careful watch on proceedings from just one behind Langer and Ballesteros. There was plenty of strong American artillery to prevent a European win but none of them could combat the coolness of Langer over the last 18 holes.

Ray Floyd lost his grip in the opening nine holes on the final day but Curtis Strange was ready to replace him at the top of the leader board and he went into a four-shot lead over the two Europeans at the ninth hole. Strange dropped his first shot of the day at the 10th and then Langer birdied what many feel is the most important hole in the back nine, the 12th. It was only his second birdie of the day but the pressure was on Strange and he started to make mistakes. He took six at the 13th after going into the lake and two holes later he found the water again. Langer birdied both those holes and walked to the 16th one up. While all this was happening, Langer's playing partner Ballesteros was struggling, particularly with his putter, and was battling to make pars, let alone pick up birdies. Langer was on his own – he just had to maintain that one-stroke lead over Strange and when he holed a 10-foot putt for a birdie at the 17th he went two up and his first 'Major' was as good as won.

Right: *Had Curtis Strange won the 1985 Masters his four rounds of 80-65-68-71 would have been the most remarkable scoreline in the history of the tournament.*

Below: *Wouldn't you have thought they would have given him a red jacket to match the trousers?*

Langer putted brilliantly throughout the tournament, only three-putting once in all 72 holes, and turned around a four-stroke deficit on the last nine holes, to a two-stroke victory. Curtis Strange nearly pulled off one of the great turnarounds after his opening 80 but, when the pressure was on, he fell to the coolness of Langer.

That coolness was to be evident in the Ryder Cup match held at Sutton Coldfield five months later when the 28-year-old German played a very important part.

1985 MASTERS

Final scores:

282	BERNHARD LANGER	72-74-68-68
284	Severiano Ballesteros	72-71-71-70
284	Ray Floyd	70-73-69-72
284	Curtis Strange	80-65-68-71

NON-AMERICAN WINNERS OF THE MASTERS

1961 Gary Player (South Africa)
1974 Gary Player (South Africa)
1978 Gary Player (South Africa)
1980 Severiano Ballesteros (Spain)
1983 Severiano Ballesteros (Spain)
1985 Bernhard Langer (West Germany)

THE FINAL NAIL IN THE COFFIN

With Ballesteros winning the Masters twice since 1980, Langer the reigning Champion, and Sandy Lyle the current British Open Champion, there was every chance the Europeans would dent American pride even further by taking the Ryder Cup off them. After all, the Australians took the America's Cup in 1983 when it looked like having its permanent home in New York. Surely the Ryder Cup couldn't leave American shores as well?

Tony Jacklin, Britain's favorite golfing son, was entrusted with the job of leading the European side at Palm Beach Gardens in 1983 and, my word, how close his team came to pulling off their first win in the States, losing by just one point. After such a struggle to hold on to the Cup they last lost in 1957, there was now, in 1985, a real possibility that the Americans could lose the trophy after a 28-year monopoly.

Right: *The experienced Fuzzy Zoeller lost all his matches in 1985; both fourballs, and the singles.*

Below: *The beautiful setting of Europe's great victory, the Belfry near Sutton Coldfield.*

coming back to win after being behind had proved an even harder task.

The Americans still led after the afternoon fourballs, but wins by youngster Paul Way and his partner Ian Woosnam, and by Ballesteros and Pinero, again, reduced the first-day arrears to just one point. Jacklin could see the enthusiasm among his team and must have been pleased with the first day's play despite trailing. Opposing captain Lee Trevino, who was at his most serious with little clowning and joking, must have been equally pleased at his one-point lead because he could see how fired-up the home team was, and not only that, he was fighting to beat two opponents – Jacklin's team, and the large partisan crowd.

While Ballesteros was proving to be the backbone of the European side, the contribution of the young, relatively inexperienced pairing of Paul Way and Ian Woosnam was also proving to be a tower of strength and a credit to Jacklin's judgment. Bernhard Langer, however, after showing the Americans a thing or two at Augusta, was struggling. After losing his opening match with Nick Faldo to Calvin Peete and Tom Kite he could only manage a half in the first day fourballs with his new partner Jose-Maria Canizares.

Above right: *Sandy Lyle had a mixed Ryder Cup in 1985, but in the end it all came right for the British Open champion.*

Right: *The huge crowd watches Mark O'Meara putt.*

Below: *The 1985 United States Ryder Cup team before the contest. There were not so many smiling faces afterward.*

Above: *Two of Europe's heroes, Ian Woosnam (putting) and Paul Way. Undaunted by their American counterparts they won both their fourball matches against the more experienced Fuzzy Zoeller and Hubert Green.*

If any man could motivate his players and lift them for the occasion, then it was Jacklin. He had seen and done it all before, and he knew what emotions players carried around in their minds. He knew when they were down and he also knew how to bring them back to reality when they were over-enthusiastic. But, despite all his pre-match team talks, only Ballesteros and Manuel Pinero could muster a win for the home side on the first morning foursomes as an all-too-familiar story unfolded with the visitors going into a 3-1 lead. Great Britain, or Europe, as the team was now, had struggled to hold on to early leads in past matches,

Above: *Bernhard Langer, obviously delighted with his putt!*

Right: *Sam Torrance encountering a bit of trouble at the 8th. It was not all gloom for the Scot as he had the honor of clinching the match for Europe.*

Jacklin found the German a third partner for the morning session on the second day when Jacklin brought Open champion Sandy Lyle back to the fray after leaving him out of the fourballs on the first day after an uninspiring performance with Ken Brown in the foursomes.

After Torrance and Clark, and Way and Woosnam had gained wins to give the home team the lead, Langer and Lyle were left to try and regain the lead after Ballesteros and Pinero went down 3 & 2 to Mark O'Meara and Lanny Wadkins to level the match again. But it looked as though the Americans would hold on to their one-point lead when Stadler and Strange led Langer and Lyle by two with two to play. Lyle, however, changed matters when he sank a monster putt from 40-feet at the 17th and then Stadler had a two-footer at the 18th to halve the hole and win the match but he missed and it proved to be the turning point of the 1985 Ryder Cup. That miss meant the teams were level at the half-way stage and tension was mounting, not only among the thousands of fans at the Belfry but among the millions of Britons and

Above, left: *The senior member of the United States team Ray Floyd, who was appearing in his sixth Ryder Cup.*

Above, right: *One of four Spaniards in the European team, Manuel Pinero.*

Below: *Peter Jacobsen did not enjoy his debut Ryder Cup, winning just one match, a foursome with Curtis Strange.*

Americans watching on their television sets.

Trevino, and indeed Jacklin, expressed sympathy at Stadler's bad fortune but despite his captain's words of encouragement Stadler could not make amends in the afternoon as he and his partner, Hal Sutton, lost heavily to Ballesteros and Pinero. The European team won three of the foursomes, with only Way and Woosnam letting them down by losing to Strange and Peter Jacobsen. It is not fair to say Way and Woosnam let the home side down because they played their part in helping secure Europe's two point lead going into the final day. Both the youngsters had matured during the last two days of intense golf.

The Americans were going into the last day in an unusual position – trailing. And Trevino must have been very

Above: *Sam Torrance's one-hole win over Andy North was enough to clinch victory for Europe. Here he plays his second to the 18th to win the match, the only time he was ahead all day.*

Left: *The successful European team. Clockwise from top left; Rivero, Langer, Faldo, Torrance, Jacklin, Lyle, Way, Ballesteros, Brown, Pinero, Canizares, Woosnam and Clark.*

much aware that the European team, built around the experience and talent of Ballesteros and Langer, was highly-motivated and the lesser-known golfers were playing to a level they had rarely reached before. Manuel Pinero continued Europe's run with a 3 & 1 win over Lanny Wadkins but Craig Stadler temporarily halted the slide with a win over Ian Woosnam. Way, however, tipped the scales once more with a two-hole win over Ray Floyd. Ballesteros and Kite halved their match and from thereon it was one European success after the other. Tony Jacklin was flitting from green to green in the hope of seeing the match-winning putt. Howard Clark had the chance to clinch the match, then Jose Rivero had his chance for glory but the final act was performed by Sam Torrance who strode up the 18th fairway with tears in his eyes knowing he had the easiest of tasks to win the hole, and the Cup, after his opponent, Andy North, put his tee shot into the lake. Torrance played the hole out and the cheers could be heard for miles around. The champagne corks popped and the rest of the match was lost amid the celebrations.

European golfers were 'born' in 1980 when Severiano Ballesteros made his breakthrough at Augusta. Their stature was confirmed at Sutton Coldfield on 15 September 1985 when the United States bid farewell to the Ryder Cup after a 28-year grip on it.

1985 RYDER CUP

GREAT BRITAIN/EUROPE SUCCESSES

1929 Moortown, Leeds	GREAT BRITAIN 7	UNITED STATES 5
1933 Southport & Ainsdale, Southport	GREAT BRITAIN 6½	UNITED STATES 5½
1957 Lindrick, Sheffield	GREAT BRITAIN 7½	UNITED STATES 4½
1985 The Belfry, Sutton Coldfield	EUROPE 16½	UNITED STATES 11½

1985 Results: (European scores first)

First Day

Foursomes
S. Ballesteros & M. Pinero beat C. Strange & M. O'Meara 2 & 1
B. Langer & N. Faldo lost to C. Peete & T. Kite 3 & 2
A. Lyle & K. Brown lost to L. Wadkins & R. Floyd 4 & 3
H. Clark & S. Torrance lost to C. Stadler & H. Sutton 3 & 2

Fourballs
P. Way & I. Woosnam beat F. Zoeller & H. Green 1 hole
S. Ballesteros & M. Pinero beat A. North & P. Jacobsen 2 & 1
B. Langer & J. M. Canizares halved with C. Stadler & H. Sutton
S. Torrance & H. Clark lost to R. Floyd & L. Wadkins 1 hole
Match score: Europe 3½ USA 4½

Second Day

Fourballs
S. Torrance & H. Clark beat T. Kite & A. North 2 & 1
P. Way & I. Woosnam beat H. Green & F. Zoeller 4 & 3
S. Ballesteros & M. Pinero lost to M. O'Meara & L. Wadkins 3 & 2
B. Langer & A. Lyle halved with C. Strange & C. Stadler

Foursomes
J. M. Canizares & J. Rivero beat T. Kite & C. Peete 7 & 5
S. Ballesteros & M. Pinero beat C. Stadler & H. Sutton 5 & 4
P. Way & I. Woosnam lost to C. Strange & P. Jacobsen 4 & 2
B. Langer & K. Brown beat R. Floyd & L. Wadkins 3 & 2
Match score: Europe 9 USA 7

Third Day

Singles
M. Pinero beat L. Wadkins 3 & 1
I. Woosnam lost to C. Stadler 2 & 1
P. Way beat R. Floyd 2 holes
S. Ballesteros halved with T. Kite
A. Lyle beat P. Jacobsen 3 & 2
B. Langer beat H. Sutton 5 & 4
S. Torrance beat A. North 1 hole
H. Clark beat M. O'Meara 1 hole
J. Rivero lost to C. Peete 1 hole
N. Faldo lost to H. Green 3 & 1
J. M. Canizares beat F. Zoeller 2 holes
K. Brown lost to C. Strange 4 & 2

THE AMERICANS COME BACK

After the doom and despondency of 1985, it was back to normal for American golf in 1986 as home-grown players won all three domestic 'Majors.' But few would have predicted the winners of these championships as, first of all, Jack Nicklaus and Ray Floyd, with 24 and 23 years professional experience respectively behind them, proved it was the year of the 'Aged' as they won the Masters and Open, and then Bob Tway, a 27-year-old from Oklahoma in just his second year on the Tour, wound up the season by taking the PGA title.

But for sheer fairytale material, Nicklaus' record sixth Masters win in April was the story of 1986 throughout the entire world of sport.

Right: *Bob Tway finished second to Greg Norman in the 1986 money list, and also won his first major, the PGA.*

Below: *Jack Nicklaus astounded his critics by winning his record sixth Masters in 1986 at the age of 46.*

Above: *Like all experienced professionals Nicklaus prepares carefully for every shot.*

1986 MASTERS

Final scores:

279 JACK NICKLAUS	74-71-69-65	280 Tom Kite	70-74-68-68
280 Greg Norman	70-72-68-70	281 Severiano Ballesteros	71-68-72-70
		282 Nick Price	79-69-63-71

NICKLAUS' SIXTH MASTERS

In his 47th year, Nicklaus had always loved playing at Augusta ever since his first Masters as an amateur in 1959. But, despite his five victories, and long love-affair with the course and championship, he had not won the title since that great championship of 1975 when he beat off Johnny Miller and Tom Weiskopf.

Nicklaus rarely plays badly at Augusta, and sometimes that is good enough to win the title, other times it is not as somebody storms through with a couple of blistering rounds to snatch the title like Ray Floyd did in 1976 and Tom Watson the following year. The 1986 event was, however, one of those occasions when Nicklaus played his usual steady four rounds and this time emerged the winner, but right out of the blue.

In all fairness to Nicklaus he had done very little leading up to the Masters to justify his inclusion in the list of favorites and a lot of attention was, naturally, focussed on the European pair of Ballesteros and Langer. Curtis Strange and Calvin Peete were regarded as the best of the home professionals and the ones most likely to be capable of breaking the European monopoly.

Augusta was at its beautiful best, and why not, because this was a special Masters – the 50th, and it was a testament to Bobby Jones' innovation that it remains one of the most prized of

Above: *Greg Norman led Nick Price, Severiano Ballesteros and Tom Kite going into the final round of the 1986 Masters, but Jack Nicklaus strode past all of them to win.*

Below: *South African Nick Price who shot a Masters record 63 in the third round.*

Right: *Had this putt gone in at the 18th Nick Price would have knocked two shots off the Masters record.*

golf's many great championships. The greens were fast, too fast for Langer and British Open champion Sandy Lyle although Ballesteros managed to master them a little better to break par with a 71. Nicklaus had a two-over par 74 but was six down on the leaders Ken Green and Bill Kratzert.

Ballesteros took the lead on the second day with a four-under 68 and managed to keep the ball under the pin for uphill putts at 16 of the 18 holes – undoubtedly the best place to be on such fast surfaces. Langer moved into contention along with Australian Greg Norman and, once more, it looked as though the Americans were going to be shut-out by the overseas invasion. For a time Tom Watson headed the home challenge but came to grief with a triple bogey six at the 12th and dropped from four-under after nine holes. Nicklaus made the cut, unlike some of his fellow old-timers Player, Palmer and Floyd, but on 145 he was six behind Ballesteros.

A real race opened up at the top of the leader board after round three with

Right: *Greg Norman topped the US money list in 1986 with $653,296.*

Below: *Severiano Ballesteros at the 18th on the second day of the 1986 Masters. He shot a four-under 68 to take the lead.*

Norman taking the lead on 210 while Ballesteros and Langer were one behind on 211. Joining the Europeans were South African Nick Price, who shot a Masters record 63, and the sole American challenger, Donnie Hammond from Daytona Beach. Nicklaus shot a third-round 69 but was four off the lead and, despite his many years of experience of big tournaments, even he could hardly have imagined what the final day had in store for him.

The Australian Norman let his lead go after errors at the eighth and tenth and these allowed Ballesteros to take the lead which he eventually increased. As he stood on the 15th tee he was three up on the new second-placed man, Nicklaus, who had crept up with a charge that was a mixture of steady pars interspersed with the odd birdie. Shortly before Ballesteros arrived at the 15th, however, Nicklaus had had an eagle three at the same hole, but the Spaniard was less fortunate as he found the water with his second shot, and he had a further disaster at the 16th when he bogeyed the hole to find his advantage suddenly wiped out. He was one down to Nicklaus who birdied the 17th and parred the last to come in with a nine-under 279. He could only sit and watch as the rest fought it out. Ballesteros could not get out of his slump, but Norman had pulled himself back into the contest, and Tom Kite had suddenly emerged as a strong challenger.

Ballesteros came home two behind Nicklaus and then Kite and Norman, in turn, had chances to level the championship on the final hole. Kite missed an 11-footer to tie and it was left to Norman but, just as at Winged Foot in 1984 when he had a chance to win the Open, he played a terrible second shot that went into the stands. He had to get down in two to stay alive but missed his ten-foot putt as Nicklaus stood by in near disbelief at winning his sixth Masters title. He had emerged from a strong field as the only one capable of breaking the overseas dominance and, at 46 years and three months he became the oldest winner of the title.

It is appropriate that in a book that has spanned seventy years of great golfers and great golfing moments, we should return to Jack Nicklaus in the final chapter as he has provided as many, if not more, great moments than any other golfer. But, if Jack could still go on winning titles in 1986 so could another old stager – Ray Floyd who, at nearly 44 years of age, became the oldest winner of the US Open.

Left: *Jack Nicklaus concludes his round, his fate is now out of his hands. Even he must have thought he was dreaming when he won.*

Above: *You would have thought Jack had something to look happy about.*

NICKLAUS' RECORD SIX MASTERS WINS

1963	1965	1966	1972	1975	1986
286 NICKLAUS	271 NICKLAUS	288 NICKLAUS	286 NICKLAUS	276 NICKLAUS	279 NICKLAUS
287 Tony Lema	280 Arnold Palmer	288 Tommy Jacobs	289 Tom Weiskopf	277 Tom Weiskopf	280 Greg Norman
	280 Gary Player	288 Gay Brewer	289 Bobby Mitchell	277 Johnny Miller	280 Tom Kite
		(Nicklaus won play-off 70-72-78)	289 Bruce Crampton		

ANOTHER OLD 'UN HAS HIS DAY

Floyd had been a winner on the US circuit since victory in the 1963 St Petersburg Open as a 20-year-old rookie yet, despite winning 'Majors' in three decades, he had never won the Open, in fact he had never figured in the top two. His last 'Major' was the 1982 PGA Championship which ended a great two-year run in which he won six Tour events and finished second on the money list in both years. A decline in his fortunes in 1983 and 1984, when he slumped to 68th on the list, was reversed in 1985 when he finished fifth in the money list and won his first tournament on the Tour for nearly three years.

He went into 1986 with a new found confidence and was in contention for the Masters title at Augusta in April, just as he had been at Augusta 12 months earlier. Despite his advancing years Floyd compensated for his ageing body with a mental maturity that had kept him a notable competitor at, or near, the top.

Shinnecock Hills was the venue for the 86th Open, the first time since 1896 that the famous course had been used for the Championship. The Long

Below left: *Ray Floyd in action at Wentworth in 1969 at the age of 27 . . .*

Below right: *. . . and how he looked 17 years later, when he won his first US Open.*

Island course, along Route 495 out of New York, was named after the Shinnecock tribe of Indians that used to inhabit part of Long Island. It is one of the oldest in America and generally reckoned to be the nearest thing to a Scottish links course in the United States.

Nicklaus went into intense preparation for the Open after his great win at Augusta and was keen to become the oldest winner of another 'Major.' Once again the overseas contingent was present in all its glory and Ballesteros, who had never won the US Open, was desperate to add it to his list of credits. He was paired with Johnny Miller in the first round and memories of that great British Open at Birkdale in 1976 came flooding back. All the glory since that day, however, had fallen upon the Spaniard and not Miller.

The bitterly cold and driving rain on the opening day developed into a near-gale as conditions became even more reminiscent of a British seaside links and, on a course that demands accuracy at the best of times, scores rocketed as survival became the name of the game. Nicklaus reckoned par should have been 77 not 70 and Bob Tway, winner of the previous week's Westchester Classic, was the only man to make par – a remarkable feat in such dreadful conditions. Norman made 71 and Ray Floyd, considering the conditions he had to play in, did well to return a 75 – two-under Nicklaus' 'par.' Conditions were so bad that Nicklaus lost a ball, the first time that had happened to him since the 1959 British Amateur championship.

Realistic scoring was restored on day two as the weather calmed down and Greg Norman took the lead at one under after a 68. Lee Trevino was three behind the Australian, also after a 68, and Floyd shot the same score to finish one behind Trevino. Joey Sindelar broke the course record with a 66 but was eight behind Norman following his first day 81. The European challenge fizzled out with Langer five off the lead, Ballesteros nine off, and Sandy Lyle ten behind Norman.

Norman held on to his lead in the third round, despite a confrontation with a drunk on the course, and was level par over three rounds. He had a

Above: *In winning the 1986 Open at the age of 44 Ray Floyd became the oldest winner of the championship.*

Right: *Another veteran who figured in the 1986 US Open was Lee Trevino but his final round of 71 was not enough to sustain his challenge.*

1986 US OPEN

Scores after round 3:

210	Greg Norman
211	Lee Trevino
211	Hal Sutton
212	Bob Tway
213	Denis Watson
213	RAY FLOYD
213	Mark McCumber
213	Payne Stewart
213	Mike Reid

Final scores:

Score	Player	Final round
279	RAY FLOYD	66
281	Chip Beck	65
281	Lanny Wadkins	65
282	Lee Trevino	71
283	Payne Stewart	70

Oldest winners of the Major Championships

Masters:	Jack Nicklaus (1986) 46 years
US Open:	Ray Floyd (1986) 43 years
British Open:	Tom Morris, Snr, (1867) 46 years
US PGA:	Julius Boros (1968) 48 years

Above: *Ray Floyd and family share his US Open win.*

Left: *After faltering in the last round of the Masters and US Open, Australian Greg Norman eventually got his reward in the British Open at Turnberry.*

one-stroke lead and was in the same position as he had been going into the final round of the Masters when Nicklaus won. Floyd was three behind the leader, which was less than Nicklaus' deficit at Augusta, but Floyd was just one of the many golfers ready to pounce if Norman faltered again as he had done in the Masters.

The final day was one of the most frantic in the history of the Open as the leader board changed time and time again with nine players sharing the lead at one stage. But the complete dedication and professionalism of Raymond Floyd, one time manager of an all-girl topless band, pulled him through as his final round of 66 edged him ahead of quality players like Lanny Wadkins, who lowered the course record with a 65, Lee Trevino, Jack Nicklaus and Bernhard Langer. Australian Greg Norman failed again at the last hurdle, but he was to have his moment of glory a month later in the British Open at Turnberry. For the time being, however, the glorious moment of winning his first Open belonged to Ray Floyd which meant the winners of the first two 'Majors' of 1986 had a combined age of 90 years. What would the Chinese call it? – 'The Year of the Geriatric!'

FROM OUIMET TO TWAY

Just as we started with a little-known golfer, Francis Ouimet, so we finish with one, Bob Tway, who made an astonishing impact during his second year on the US Tour.

It would, however, have been nice to have finished by recalling the elusive Grand Slam – the winning of all four 'Majors' in one year – as Australian Greg Norman came as close as any golfer in recent times to the achievement that has eluded all the great golfers. But Jack Nicklaus deprived him at Augusta and Ray Floyd did so at Shinnecock Hills. Norman did have his one moment of triumph and thus rid himself of the 'nearly man' tag at Turnberry when he won the British Open. At the Inverness Club, Toledo, he came close once more before losing to the 27-year Oklahoman Tway.

Tway was little known until 1986. He had finished 46th on the money list in his first year, 1985 (in fact $500 behind Jack Nicklaus!). But, if Nicklaus could rise from that position to win the Masters then perhaps Tway could do likewise in the PGA championship. The 1986 season indeed proved to be a good one for Tway who had notched up three wins before the PGA Championship to rise from obscurity to second in the money list, albeit $100,000 behind Norman.

The entire 1985 European Ryder Cup-winning team was invited to compete at Inverness and all accepted except Sandy Lyle, Jose Rivero, and Sam Torrance. The European and Australian contingent was the strongest gathering from overseas for any US PGA event and Langer and Ballesteros

Above: *'It's hard work winning' . . . Bob Tway the 1986 PGA champion.*

Left: *Greg Norman doesn't look too happy during the 1986 PGA championship. He has thrown away another chance of victory.*

were very much in evidence as they were keen to add a European name to the list of 'Majors' for 1986. Such a name had been missing from the three 'Majors' already decided and it was five years since no European had had his name engraved on any one of the four coveted trophies.

Inverness was playing host to its first PGA Championship, although it had hosted the US Open four times. The most characteristic features of Inverness are its small, tight, greens and Bob Tway said before the championship: 'If you don't find the fairways, you don't find the greens.'

It was Norman who set the tournament alight on the opening day with a course record 65 with one of his best displays of long, accurate driving. He built up a two-shot lead over Phil Blackmar and Craig Stadler, who had won the 1973 Amateur championship at Inverness. The European challenge was not to be seen and the best came from Ian Woosnam and Howard Clark who both shot 72s, the same as Tway.

Never far from the limelight, Jack Nicklaus, playing in his 100th 'Major,' shot a second-round 68 to take a share of the lead for a time with Peter Jacobsen on 138 before Norman added a 68 to his opening round for a 133. Norman's four-stroke lead over Payne Stewart and Mike Hulbert equalled the PGA record after two rounds but remarkably none of the other men who had enjoyed such a lead, Tommy Aaron (1967), Gil Morgan (1976) and Tom Watson (1978), went on to win the title. And, after Norman's tendency to 'blow up' it should have served as an omen to him.

Norman held his four stroke lead after the third round to create a record by becoming the first man to lead after three rounds in all four 'Majors' in one year, but that lead would have been

Below: *Bob Tway playing a long iron at Inverness on his way to his first major title.*

greater if Tway had not blitzed his way up the leader board with a record 64, just one off the record for any 'Major.'

So, the final day of the final 'Major' of 1986 was down to the top two money winners – Norman and Tway. At 2.30 pm, however, after both had hit their drives at the second, play was suspended by the PGA because of the appalling weather conditions. Thirteen of the final 73 starters had completed their round and Hale Irwin was the leader in the club house on 287, but knew he had no chance of winning the title. Play was put back until the Monday, only the second time since the Championship became a medal event that play was delayed. The last occasion was in 1976 when Dave Stockton won at the Congressional Club in Maryland.

When play resumed, Tway played spectacular golf to save pars and make birdies, while a double bogey at the 11th and a bogey at the 14th cost Norman dearly. They were level going into the 18th after a great day's golf. Both hit good drives but Tway found the bunker with his second while Norman hit the green but saw the ball spin off the back and into thickish rough. Tway chipped into the cup from the bunker for a birdie and the Championship had been won with a birdie at the 18th, the first time that had happened since the event became a stroke-play event in 1958. Norman made a bogey to crown what could be described as a bad year for him . . . a strange description for a man who headed the money list and won the British Open. But he had three glorious chances of winning the other 'Majors' and threw them all away.

As for Tway, he is the last name we encounter on our seventy-year trip down memory lane, but as Nicklaus and Floyd have shown in 1986, winning can go on for years, and Bob Tway could very easily install himself alongside many of the great names we have encountered as one of golf's immortals.

1986 US PGA

Final scores:	
276 BOB TWAY	72-70-64-70
278 Greg Norman	65-68-69-76
279 Peter Jacobsen	68-70-70-71
280 D. A. Weibring	72-71-68-69

Left: *'The Great White Shark,' Greg Norman, unleashes an iron during the PGA championship.*

Overleaf: *Bob Tway, the latest in the long list of major championship winners. But that list will not end at Tway.*

INDEX

Page numbers in *italics* refer to illustrations

Picture Credits

All-Sport: pages 3, 6, 65 (bottom right) 66, 73 (bottom), 74 (left), 77 (top), 84-85, 89, 90 (bottom), 96, 102, 110, 111, 116 (both), 117 (bottom), 120 (both), 121 (both), 122 (bottom), 124 (both), 125 (both top), 128 (both), 129, 130 (top), 131, 132 (top), 133, 134, 135 (right), 137, 138 (top), 139 (right), 140, 141, 142.

Associated Press: pages 20, 26 (both), 27, 28, 39 (bottom), 40, 46 (both), 58 (bottom), 60 (right), 62, (bottom), 64 (top & bottom), 68 (top), 69 (both), 75 (bottom), 78, 81 (top), 90 (top), 94 (top), 114 (bottom).

BBC Hulton: pages 6, 11 (all pictures), 12, 13 (top & bottom), 14, 14-15, 15, 16 (bottom), 17 (all pictures), 18 (top & bottom), 19, 22 (both), 24, 24-25, 31 (bottom right), 36-37, 39 (top), 48, 52, 57, 58 (top), 60, 71 (both), 83, 86, 104.

BBC Hulton/Bettman Archive: pages 9 (top), 16 (top), 21, 29 (top), 32, 33, 35 (left), 45, 47, 55 (left), 92.

Brian Morgan, Golf Photography International: pages 7 (bottom), 9 (bottom), 113 (top), 114 (top), 115, 118, 119 (both), 122 (top), 123 (bottom), 125 (bottom), 126 (top), 130 (bottom), 132 (bottom), 136, 139 (left).

The Bert Neale Collection pages: 8 (right), 29 (bottom), 31 (top right), 37, 38, 42, 43, 49, 50 (top), 51 (both), 55 (both), 58 (centre), 60 (left), 65 (bottom left & top), 68 (bottom), 72, 73 (top), 74 (right), 75 (top), 77 (bottom left), 79 (top), 80, 82, (both), 87, 88 (both), 91, 93 (both), 94 (bottom), 95, 97, 98, 99, 101 (bottom), 103 (both), 105 (both), 106, 107, 112, 113 (bottom), 135 (left).

TPS/Central Press: page 79 (bottom).

TPS/Keystone: pages 1, 34, 35 (center), 41, 70, 77

The Scotsman Publications Ltd: pages 56, 67 (bottom), 100, 101 (top).

Sport & General: pages 67 (top), 81 (bottom).

Bob Thomas Sports Photography: pages 7 (top), 117 (top), 123 (top), 126 (bottom), 138 (bottom).

US Golf Association: pages 23 (both, 31 (left), 35 (right), 44, 50 (bottom), 62 (top), 63.

Jacket Pictures
Front jacket, top left: Bert Neale
Front jacket, lower left: Brian Morgan
Other jacket pictures: All-Sport